PAINTING THE TWO WHITE LINES

A life-changing look at the
Commands of Christ.

Copyright ©1999 by Mark S. Schaufler
All rights reserved
Printed in the United States of America
Library of Congress Control Number 99-076355
International Standard Book Number 1-886904-38-3

MST Ministries
P.O. Box 8490
Lacey, WA 98509-8490

Printed in the USA by Morris Publishing
3212 E. Hwy 30 Kearney, NE 68847
800-650-7888

Table of Contents

Introduction...…........4

Realities of the Road.....................................…………7

8-Idealism to Reality ~ 12-Rule One-Mercy ~ 14-Rule
Two-The Learning Curve ~ 19-Rule Three-Grace ~ 22-
Rule Four-Faith ~ 26-Two White Lines

Painting the First White Line......................…..29

30-How you Listen ~ 33-Trouble and Fear ~ 37-Take My
Yoke ~ 39-His seed, His Havest ~ 42-Caught in the Act ~
45-When You Pray ~ 49-How You Pray ~ 53-Because You
Pray ~ 56-When You Fast ~ 60-How You Fast ~
64-Because You Fast ~ 68-When You Give ~ 75-How You
Give ~ 78-Because You Give ~ 82-When You Worship ~
84-How You Worship ~ 87-Because You Worship ~ 89-
When You're Tempted ~ 92-How You're Tempted ~ 94-
Because You're Tempted ~ 97-Stay on the Path ~ 100-
Open for Business ~ 102-Everything and Anything ~ 104-
Being Perfect

Painting the Second White Line...................…...107

108-Love Your ~ 110-The Dangers of Love ~ 112-Love
Not Lust~ 115-Love Your Neighbor as Yourself ~ 118-If
You Love One Another ~ 120-Love Lost-Divorce~ 123-
Love Your Enemies ~ 126-When You're Angry~ 128-How
You're Angry~ 132-Because You're Angry~ 134-Howdy
Stranger ~ 136-Judge "Not" ~ 139-Look Ma! No Plank! ~

Painting the Second White Line~Continued

141-You Flunked What? ~ 144-People versus Possessions ~ 147-People versus Position ~ 149-Do Something 152-When Things Don't Change ~ 155-The Heart Monitor ~ 158-Mission Field or Missionary

Ministry..162

163-Follow Me ~ 165-The Message ~ 167-The Pace-Love the Children ~ 170-Clothed With Power ~ 172-Get Ready ~ 175-Go! ~ 177-Greater Things ~ 180-Guess Who's Coming to Dinner? ~ 182-Made for Miracles ~ 185-Rest ~ 187-"Listen" ~ 189-Bottom of the 9th ~ 192-Saying "Yes" When EverthingWithin You Cries "No." ~ 194-Do Not Be Afraid ~ 197-Lazarus, come out! ~ 199-You Deaf and Mute Spirit! ~ 202-When it is More that a Headache ~ 206-Healed ~ 209-Home-Town Obstacles ~ 211-Evangelism-Seekers ~ 214-Evangelism-Seek Them ~ 216-Mercy Ministry ~ 219-Others-Unity ~ 222-Woe to Religion ~ 225-The Sabbath ~ 228-Forgiveness From God ~ 231-Doubting, Again ~ 233-If They Hate You ~ 235-Tough Times Ahead ~ 237-Quitting Time ~ 241-Baptize and Teach 243-Last Thoughts

Scripture Reference Section.....................244

Introduction

It has been over twenty years since I said "yes" to Jesus and began to follow Him. Many things about those early years have remained the same. The Bible is a consistent challenge, the world is in constant need, God's forgiveness continues, and I cry in the presence of a Holy God.

Other things have changed. Optimism has been replaced by faith. God is bigger than He was at first and we are much smaller. His word is much more important than I realized. His way is not just an option; it is the only hope anyone has of living a life that matters. And ALL of His ways and commands need to be a part of our daily lives.

In my journey with Christ, numerous people have helped me. Some of them are friends and still help today. Others were authors that I will never meet. I say thank you to all of them. Their contributions have been priceless.

Now it is my turn to pass on to others some of the things that have been given to me; to us. Jesus' last words in Matthew have been called the Great Commission. As a part of that we are called to "**Therefore go and make disciples of all nations, baptizing them in the name of the Father and of the Son and of the Holy Spirit, and** teaching them to obey everything I have commanded you." Matthew 28:19-20a

This book is a collection of **everything Jesus has commanded us.** His commands are organized, explained, and applied to the day we live in. His words need to become our ways. If they do, we have an opportunity to see a very biblical lifestyle lived out in any age. If they don't, then we will see all the warnings of scripture come true in our own lives.

We can not escape the realities of gravity nor can we escape the consequences of ignoring the commands of Christ. Fortunately, the commands of Christ are easier to understand than the complex gravity calculations needed to put a man on the moon. Christ's commands will also take us much farther than the moon; heaven itself will be our landing place.

You can read this book much quicker than you can apply it, so don't expect a quick transformation of your life. Read this book so that as you face life's decisions, the Holy Spirit will have something to remind you of **("But the counselor, the Holy Spirit, whom the Father will send in my name, will teach you all things and will remind you of everything I have said to you." John 14:26).** If you haven't read what Christ said, the Holy Spirit can't remind you. Use it as a daily devotional. Work through it with a Bible study group. Memorize some of the key scriptures in each section. Preach it to the people in your care.

Above all else be amazed and cherish the truth that God has given us. His truth brings a freedom to us; a freedom to live Godly lives that impact an ungodly world. What a privilege we have; what opportunities we possess!

THANK YOU!

Many thanks to Cynthia Holmes for her meticulous work in proofing and editing this volume. More thanks to my wife Kristy and the kids who help proof the application of these scriptures every day. Thank you for your support. Limitless thanks go to the Father, Son, and Holy Spirit who gave us the book we call the Bible and the life that we learn from it.

Realities
of the Road

Idealism to Reality

As long as I have been of legal driving age, I have lived near military bases and have heard numerous stories of a drivers' paradise called the Autobahn. A place where cars can legally go ... well ... faster than I had ever driven. So when my opportunity came to drive those roads, I was full of mixed emotions. Exhilaration and terror seemed to occupy my heart. Ideally I liked the idea of going very, very fast. Realistically I knew how scary traffic could be at half those speeds.

At the airport we picked up the car that would propel us down the Autobahn at racetrack speeds. It was the most expensive car I had ever driven. I took a lot of time determining where all the necessary gauges, accessories, and signals were. Looking for something on the dash at over a hundred miles an hour didn't sound too appealing.

Once I was comfortable with the layout of the car, we headed for the Autobahn. From the airport we only had a few hundred yards before we entered the in-town Autobahn. It has a speed limit of eighty miles an hour. In minutes we were on the open road with no limits. Within fifteen minutes from the time I started the car, we were going over one hundred miles an hour in moderate traffic.

Shocked, I continued to drive and eventually take the car up to its legal limit of one hundred and twenty. Shocked, because it was so easy. Shocked, because the drivers were better at these speeds on the Autobahn then we are at home at half the speeds. Shocked, because the road conditions never endangered the car's progress or speed. Shocked, because the car performed so well that I didn't have any sense that I was endangering anyone.

Three thousand safe miles later, we returned the car and flew home. There was no temptation to go that fast on our highways in my car. Neither the road, my car, nor the others on our highways could handle it. I used to think we had some of the best roads in the world. Now I have to limit that concept to our own country. I was also sad. Sad that we had settled for a standard that was so much lower than it needed to be.

As a new Christian I remember reading the words of Christ. They challenged every fiber that was me. I read the book of Acts, and wondered how that could be. There was a temptation to stop where I was and just enjoy the salvation that Jesus had given me. Forgiveness was great and now I had a new group of friends who did not do all the things that my old friends did. I could have stopped there; a lot of people do. But I didn't and you don't have to either.

Christ's commands have become my daily direction and I have been a part of numerous accounts that would fit in the book of Acts. How did I get from there to here? How can you?

John said it. Jesus said it. Peter said it. Paul said it. We need to hear it: repent! Father God has a gift for us called life. You can't squeeze it in on Sunday. Five minutes of prayer before work won't make it happen. You have to repent so that there will be space for it. Repent?

He went into all the country around the Jordan, preaching a baptism of repentance for the forgiveness of sins. As it is written in the book of the words of Isaiah the prophet: "A voice of one calling in the desert, 'Prepare the way for the Lord, make straight paths for him. Every valley shall be filled in, every mountain and hill made low. The crooked roads shall become straight, the rough ways smooth. And all mankind will see God's salvation.'" Luke 3:3-6

On the Autobahn there were no steep hills, crooked roads, deep valleys, or rough ways. The builders had leveled the landscape to accommodate the road. Then they had taken the time to build the road for the anticipated speeds. Too often in our lives we change the road to accommodate the landscape. So our roads take a sharp turn at Old McDonald's farm, bump our way along the hillside, then plummet down into the valley where we will follow the river's winding path. That is easier and quicker to build, but we will pay for it for the rest of our driving lives.

We traveled three thousand miles in seventeen days. At sixty miles an hour, that is fifty hours. At one hundred miles an hour, that is thirty hours. So we had twenty more hours to vacation than we would have had in the USA. If we had Autobahns in the USA, I could use about two hundred hours a year in other ways. How much time does your lifestyle waste?

Repentance means you change whatever needs to be changed. Jesus tells us what needs to change with His commands. That clears a path as far as you can see. If we work His commands into our lives, we will pave that path and paint the boundary lines we need to safely travel this new life. As we are faithful and mature, we will gain the capacity to go full speed on our personal Autobahn. Each car in Europe is rated for safety. A commission tests the car and gives it a top speed. Our car could go one hundred and twenty legally. Other, more expensive, cars could go even faster. You get what you pay for. Maturity has a price.

"Therefore everyone who hears these words of mine and puts them into practice is like a wise man who built his house on the rock. The rain came down, the streams rose, and the winds blew and beat against that house; yet it did not fall because it had its foundation on the rock." Matthew 7:24-25 If roads had been common and cars were invented, it might have been said this way, *"Therefore everyone who hears these words of mine and puts them into practice will be like the Germans who built Autobahns. You will be able to get where you need to go no matter what the terrain or climate throws at you. And as you are faithful in following my ways, you get to upgrade your car at every trade-in point."*

Repentance is a daily occurrence. You stumble when you do something your way instead of Christ's way; you need to repent and do it His way. Something in your past says do it another way; you need to repent and do it His way. You respond to a situation the way they do in the movies; repent and do it Christ's way. Repentance is an attitude that we adopt when we first start to follow Christ and will continue to need until the day we die. Repent! **For we are God's workmanship, created in Christ Jesus to do good works, which God prepared in advance for us to do. Ephesians 2:10** Repent and give God the space He needs to make it possible.

Rule One-Mercy

"**For the wages of sin is death.**" **Romans 6:23a** I'm alive. You're alive. Yet the scripture is still true; **the wages of sin is death.** We are still alive because "mercy" describes one of the attributes of God. Mercy means we don't get what we deserve, when we deserve it. That allows us the time it takes to repent, build, and drive.

We don't need to fear instant death from heaven. Yes, you will still pay a price for your sins. Yes, you may still have some consequences from previous sin. But God won't destroy you in disgust because of your immaturity. You've been adopted into His family and that is a very secure position.

Sin still has wages. For most sins we receive our wages on the payment plan. There may be an awkward moment. If left unresolved, it can lead to the death of a relationship. Unchecked, you may lose an opportunity for the future. You may lose a night's sleep if it continues. Your church attendance and Bible reading will suffer a slow death. Each funeral is intended to warn you. Warn you that **the wages of sin is death.**

In the financial world, the payment plan is designed to give you what you want, when you want it, at payments you can afford. When it comes to sin-don't be fooled by the similarities. You sin and you don't die. At this point you may think, "Maybe I can afford this." You may even think, "Maybe this isn't that big of a deal with God." Sometimes people call them a "pet sin." The two words "pet" and "sin" don't go together and time will prove you wrong. Once the payments start coming they don't stop-- unless you repent.

As you work your way through Christ's commands, you will find that Jesus defines sin in some very specific ways. He does that to protect us from those wages. His commands won't tell us to stop after we have already built up a head of steam on the road; they say stop before we turn the key to the engine.

Leaving any of Christ's commands out of your life will leave a stretch of unpaved roadway without boundary lines. Future trouble can probably be traced to neglected commands and the rough terrain that creates. Don't limit what God would have for your life because you stopped changing. At numerous altar times I have prayed with people who stopped growing, stopped applying Christ's commands. They are usually at the altar because something has died or is dying. The repair they need for the road is obedience. Jesus gave us the commands to protect us, to nurture us. They guide us in our growth or become signposts for our demise.

For the wages of sin is death, but the gift of God is eternal life in Christ Jesus our Lord. Romans 6:23 Keep opening the gifts that each command of Christ represents. They will pave the way to the eternal life that awaits us. God's mercy will protect our backs as long as we are moving forward. If we ever decide to turn around and exit this new highway, be prepared for the worst: the full payment of sin.

Rule Two-
The Learning Curve

"Therefore everyone who hears these words of mine and puts them into practice is like a wise man who built his house on the rock. The rain came down, the streams rose, and the winds blew and beat against the house; yet it did not fall, because it had its foundation on the rock." Matthew 7:24-25

Putting Christ's words *"into practice"* is the task before us. Some of His commands will be tougher than others. Each one of us will have good days and bad days. As Peter was learning to put Christ's words into practice, he demonstrated for us some of the key lessons we need to learn. His example will also show us how our teachers (Father God, Lord Jesus, and the Holy Spirit) will respond to our attempts.

"Come," he said. Then Peter got down out of the boat, walked on the water and came toward Jesus. But when he saw the wind, he was afraid and, beginning to sink, cried out, "Lord, save me!" Immediately Jesus reached out his hand and caught him. "You of little faith," he said, "Why did you doubt?" Matthew 14:29-31

Peter had another new experience following Jesus. We would call it a failure. More accurately, it represents the process of putting Christ's words *"into practice."* Peter did obey; good! He obeyed for several steps; great! Then he took his eyes off Jesus and looked at the wind; mistake. When fear struck, he failed. In that intense fear, he experienced the helping hand of Jesus and the straightforward reason why he failed: doubt.

You can be ashamed of your failures or you can learn from them. Peter learned. First, if Jesus asks you to do it, it can be done. Second, fear is an enemy of faith. Third, Jesus helps you even when you fail Him. Fourth, He will tell you what the real issues are (in this case, faith).

Enjoyable? No. **No discipline (training) seems pleasant at the time, but painful. Later on, however, it produces a harvest of righteousness and peace for those who have been trained by it. Hebrews 12:11 Our fathers disciplined us for a little while as they thought best; but God disciplines (trains) us for our good, that we may share in his holiness. Hebrews 12:10**

Simon Peter answered, "You are the Christ, the Son of the living God." Jesus replied, "Blessed are you, Simon son of Jonah, for this was not revealed to you by man, but by my Father in heaven." Matthew 16:16-17 Peter had heard the voice of God. It wasn't audible, but it had echoed in his heart and Peter knew something because God told him. Learning to hear God's voice is a lesson we will all learn and continue to learn as we face the growing challenges of life.

Peter took him aside and began to rebuke him. "Never, Lord!" he said. "This shall never happen to you!" Jesus turned and said to Peter, "Get behind me, Satan! You are a stumbling block to me; you do not have in mind the things of God, but the things of men." Matthew 16:22-23 Just six verses later Peter goes from being the hero of the group to the outcast. He learned he could hear God's voice. He also learned that not every thought he had was from God. Twice now we have seen Peter stumble through Christ's commands. We will see more, but remember this; Peter had repented. He wasn't trying to protect a reputation. He wasn't trying to prove anything. He had cleared the property of his life and was building a highway according to the master's plan. Peter modeled an element of learning that we must adopt in order to put *"into practice"* Christ's commands: humility.

Walking on water and hearing from God are all a part of the supernatural world. Learning to live in that realm will take some time. Don't rush it and don't ever let go of the humility that Peter continues to model for us in the next example.

While Peter was below in the courtyard, one of the servant girls of the high priest came by. When she saw Peter warming himself, she looked closely at him.

"You also were with that Nazarene, Jesus," she said.

But he denied it. "I don't know or understand what you're talking about," he said, and went out into the entryway.

When the servant girl saw him there, she said again to those standing around, "This fellow is one of them." Again he denied it.

After a little while, those standing near said to Peter, "Surely you are one of them, for you are a Galilean."

He began to call down curses on himself, and he swore to them, "I don't know this man you're talking about."

Immediately the rooster crowed the second time. Then Peter remembered the word Jesus had spoken to him: "Before the rooster crows twice you will disown

me three times." And he broke down and wept. **Mark 14:66-72**

Jesus had predicted that Peter would do that very thing: disown Christ three times (Mark 14:30). Jesus had also warned all of His disciples months earlier, **"If anyone is ashamed of me and my words in this adulterous and sinful generation, the Son of Man will be ashamed of him when he comes in his Father's glory with the holy angels." Mark 8:38**

Peter's tears came from deep within. He had sinned. As far as he understood, it was a sin with consequences he could not bear. But with the depth of his sin came the opportunity to know the depth of Christ's forgiveness. **"It is true! The Lord has risen and has appeared to Simon." Luke 24:34**

Weeks later at the Day of Pentecost a crowd of thousands were on hand when the disciples were baptized in the Holy Spirit. This crowd focused their attention on the disciples and the new noise from heaven that was **"declaring the wonders of God in our own tongue!" Acts 2:11b**

Peter stood up with the other disciples and preached the first sermon and gave the first altar call. **Peter replied, "Repent and be baptized, every one of you, in the name of Jesus Christ for the forgiveness of your sins. And you will receive the gift of the Holy Spirit. The promise is for you and your children and for all who are far off--for all whom the Lord our God will call."**

With many other words he warned them; and he pleaded with them, "Save yourselves from this corrupt generation." Those who accepted his message were baptized, and about three thousand were added to their number that day. Acts 2:38-41

Peter could preach it because Peter had experienced forgiveness. As I travel and preach, I find common needs within the church; forgiveness is one of them. Many people who attend churches are convinced that at least some of their sin isn't forgiven. Others are too ashamed to deal with sin issues so they carry that sin and God's conviction everywhere that they go.

If church attendees struggle with forgiveness, imagine what people outside of the church think. Forgiveness is a lesson you must learn before you can pass it on to the next murderer or adulterer you meet. Peter became the early leader of the church because he had learned that lesson and so many others. Learn to put Christ's words *"into practice."* It will pave your path and allow you to show the way to others.

Rule Three-Grace

For I am the least of the apostles and do not even deserve to be called an apostle, because I persecuted the church of God. But by the grace of God I am what I am, and his grace to me was not without effect. No, I worked harder than all of them--yet not I, but the grace of God that was with me. 1 Corinthians 15:9-10

To keep me from becoming conceited because of these surpassingly great revelations, there was given me a thorn in my flesh, a messenger of Satan, to torment me. Three times I pleaded with the Lord to take it away from me. But he said to me, "My grace is sufficient for you, for my power is made perfect in weakness." Therefore I will boast all the more gladly about my weaknesses, so that Christ's power may rest on me. That is why for Christ's sake, I delight in weaknesses, in insults, in hardships, in persecutions, in difficulties. For when I am weak, then I am strong. 2 Corinthians 12:7-10

Gas stations were all along the Autobahn. Traveling at high speeds does affect your gas mileage, so you had to fill up regularly. Covering so many miles so quickly also meant you needed gas no matter how great a gas mileage you were getting. At each stop you were exposed to another shock. Gas was about four dollars a gallon.

You could easily spend a hundred dollars a day for gas. If you were a penny pincher and this was just too much for you to spend, then you would be happier driving in the USA where the gas is cheaper and you can't go as far in a day. Don't be a penny pincher when it comes to God's grace.

In the gas stations you also got to look at the cars that were going slower or faster than you were. Every one of them had to come in for gas, too. Grace is the gas for the life Jesus calls us to live. No matter how mature you are or immature you are, you need the grace of God. Grace enables you to go forward in obedience. No gas; no go. No grace; no obedience.

Paul understood grace. We see him explaining grace so we would learn to live in it. He said it enabled him to do what Jesus wanted him to do the way He wanted him to do it. Paul had to move in the direction of obedience, but when he did the grace of God enabled him to obey. Paul even said that this **"grace"** was like **"Christ's power."** Paul went the extra mile because he knew that whatever he contributed would be increased by the grace of God.

If you invest in a good stock and double or triple your money, you wish you had invested even more in the first place. You gave what you had and didn't do anything else and it grew in value. Grace takes whatever you give and increases its effectiveness. So give all you can and watch it go farther than you could imagine. Grace is such a needed gift that we are encouraged to get it on a regular basis.

Let us then approach the throne of grace with confidence, so that we may receive mercy and find grace to help us in our time of need. Hebrews 4:16 Don't economize on God. He has given us a credit card for grace. Use it. Jesus already paid for it. Move forward in obedience to Christ's commands. Some of them will be easier than others. For all of them that don't come easily, get God's grace. The time you spend in His presence will refresh you and prepare you for obedience. In fact, the day will come when you say what Paul said, **'by the grace of God I am what I am, and his grace to me was not without effect. No, I worked harder than all of them--- yet not I, but the grace of God that was with me.'**

With God's grace you don't ever have to say, "I can't." You only need to say, "I haven't yet."

Rule Four-Faith

Now faith is being sure of what we hope for and certain of what we do not see. This is what the ancients were commended for. Hebrews 11:1-2 By faith ... Abel ... Enoch ... Noah ... Abraham ... Jacob ... Joseph ... Moses ... Gideon ... David ... made specific decisions and conquered impossible situations. **Hebrews chapter 11.**

At some point in your obedience to Jesus you will find some options on the road that you are traveling. Some people become missionaries. Others devote their lives to youth, children's or pastoral ministry. Evangelists travel the world with no consistent financial backing. People give large sums of money to specific projects. Individuals quit their high-paying jobs to pursue a project where no finances are visible.

In times of need, people seek prayer from others and see God answer with miracles, healings and supernatural strength and comfort. While facing some of the toughest settings life can offer they are calm and helping those in less critical situations.

Why do people do these things? How does it work? Faith. **Consequently, faith comes from hearing the message, and the message is heard through the word of Christ. Romans 10:17** As you move forward in God's grace, He will begin to specialize your life. He will do that by the specific things that He speaks to you. It will involve finances, work opportunities, people groups, countries and the decisions you make on a regular basis.

If you read through Hebrews chapter eleven, you see the individuals that make up most of the stories in the Old Testament. Each paragraph about an individual begins with the statement, **'by faith.'** They did what they did because God had given them that task to do, and they knew it was from God; that is faith.

As you are faced with life's decisions, you will have the opportunity to learn about faith. When a command of Christ addresses the situation, then you obey; by faith you are doing it God's way. If there isn't a specific command, then you should ask, "God, what do I do now?" His answer to you will be what you base your actions on; that's faith.

For years I volunteered in a local church in a children's ministry. My paying job took about fifty hours a week so I could give about five hours to the ministry. As I continued to grow in my obedience to Christ's commands, I found that those five hours of ministry and preparation became more and more important. Soon I was thinking of other ways I could minister. I came up with a logical plan. I quit work and now I had an additional fifty hours to devote to ministry. That was logical, but it wasn't by faith. God had not asked me to do that-yet.

So we depleted our savings and eventually I had to get another job. This time I took a job that paid half as much and I worked fewer hours. But I took this job **"by faith."** God had asked me to work there. I felt like going back to my old job. My old boss left me a standing offer, "your original job and a dollar an hour raise." If my old job paid a $1000 a month, my new one only paid $360. Logically, we should have had financial trouble. Yet in the next year and a half, we paid for the birth of our first baby with cash; we had no insurance. I bought and paid for a ministerial study course. We vacationed with friends in California. And we learned a number of lessons about faith.

We live by faith, not by sight. 2 Corinthians 5:7 Biblical faith begins with God. It is His directives for our lives that guide us; not the circumstances that we see. So our unseen God calls to us and we obey; that is faith. Paul experienced that on a regular basis in the adventures he experienced as a missionary. **So keep up your courage, men, (they had been caught in a raging storm on a boat for many days) for I have faith in God that it will happen just as he told me. Acts 27:25**

So as you are traveling down the road that Christ's commands make for you, remember that your decisions need to have their origin with Him. If you don't ask for His wisdom on your decisions, you run the potential of living life by sight and not by faith. If that happens, you have violated one of the rules of the road and may well end up driving through the jungles that are on either side of the pavement.

Ready to Pave and Paint?

This is a life long project. God has the patience to work with you on it. Will you take Him at His word and work with Him?

Two White Lines

You were running a good race. Who cut in on you and kept you from obeying the truth? Galatians 5:7 Two white lines keep you in your lane on a running track. Christ's commands paint those same two white lines on the autobahn that His commands pave. If we stay between the lines, we won't cut anyone else off nor be stopped for long when somebody else cuts into our lane. Without the two white lines we will be like swerving drunks on the highway as we endanger ourselves and all those around us.

"Teacher, which is the greatest commandment in the Law?" Jesus replied: "'Love the Lord your God with all your heart and with all your soul and with all your mind. This is the first and greatest commandment. And the second is like it: 'Love your neighbor as yourself.' All the Law and the Prophets hang on these two commandments." Matthew 22:36-40
These two commandments, the two white lines, will keep us in our lane on the highway. Staying between the lines means that we will make progress and be able to work with those who are on the same highway with us. Jesus could have preached just three sermons. Repent. Love God. Love people. But He said a lot more than that. Why? He needed to define the word **'Love'** for us. Love

takes on its real meaning only in the light and direction that Christ's commands provide.

I have done surveys in a variety of settings. The most unusual experience came when I asked people this seemingly simple question, "If you were writing a dictionary, how would you define the word 'Love?'" What I heard saddened me. No one had a good answer. Most people didn't have any answer at all. Others would respond with a statement, "I don't think there is such a thing; I've never seen it." It is no wonder that Jesus gave us so many commandments to define love. He is dealing with something we don't understand.

Two other key words need to be examined in this passage as well: *"all"* and *"neighbor."*

"All" means everything; a 100% effort. If I take *"all"* of my money out of the bank, that means I don't have a penny there anymore. If I ate *"all"* of the ice cream, that means I licked the container clean. If I did *"all"* the push-ups I could do, then a billion dollars couldn't get me to do one more. This word *"all"* is a big word with many implications.

If we *"love the Lord our God with all"* then we have held nothing back and moved forward with everything. There is no other plan that we hold on to just in case this doesn't work. It is consistent with the call to repent. You give Him your *"all"* and He replaces it with His *"all."*

"Neighbor" needs definition as well. In Luke 10:29-37 Jesus defined a *"neighbor."* He used a story we call the "Good Samaritan," from it we can see Christ's application for today.

There are more people in need today than ever before. There are homeless people in thousands of locations worldwide. Hunger takes more lives than we can imagine. The list of victims of crime and war (like the man in Jesus' story) grows daily. We know this because we see it in the news every day.

Does Jesus expect us to solve *"all"* the world's problems ourselves? No and Yes. The story of the "Good Samaritan" involves a man who helped in a situation that he stumbled upon in his local area. No, that story doesn't tell us that the world is our neighbor. Yes, Jesus does expect us to change the world because he will send his people *"all"* over the globe.

What your life holds involves the two white lines that Christ's commands will define for you. As you learn to obey these commands you will accomplish God's will for your location. In time He may ask you to go somewhere else and live between the white lines and help others to do the same thing. That may make you a pastor, a missionary, or an evangelist.

Beware of the trap of hopelessness that these overwhelming problems can generate in your heart. If you stay between the lines you will make a difference in this dying world. If you don't, you won't. You will only become another one of the statistics.

We have a map for this new highway. Jesus drew it Himself as He lived His life. We have this map in the Bible. **Therefore, since we are surrounded by such a great cloud of witnesses, let us throw off everything that hinders and the sin that so easily entangles, and let us run with perseverance the race marked out for us. Let us fix our eyes on Jesus, the author and perfecter of our faith, who for the joy set before him endured the cross, scorning its shame, and sat down at the right hand of the throne of God. Consider him who endured such opposition from sinful men, so that you will not grow weary and lose heart. Hebrews 12:1-3**

Painting The First White Line

"Love the Lord your God with all your heart and with all your soul and with all your mind."

Matthew 22:37

How You Listen

When he (Jesus) said this, he called out, "He who has ears to hear, let him hear." Luke 8:8b My ears do a good job of holding my glasses in the right spot. Some ears are a walking jewelry store. Other ears make a great conversation piece. Certain ears have not seen the sun in years.

Most of us still have our ears, but are they ears to hear? Listening is a lost art for many people. You talk to them but they aren't listening. Yes, they are looking at you. They may even nod their heads at the right times. Listening? No.

Listening is the first step towards action. Everything we hear requires some kind of a response. We know that. So we turn off our ears because there is so much being said. If the normal person tried to respond to everything that they hear on the radio, newspaper, TV, news, business talk, home talk, and thought life, they would need a day with one hundred hours in it. Therefore, we become very selective in what we hear among the thousands of bytes that we listen to.

Too often that selection process becomes so automatic that we don't hear what God might be saying to us. Jesus had to ask the people then, do you have *"ears to hear?"* He could ask the same question today.

Therefore consider carefully how you listen. Whoever has will be given more: whoever does not have, even what he thinks he has will be taken from him. Luke 8:18

As Jesus speaks to us through His written word, will we listen? Will we begin a response that leads to action? Remember it is a part of the master plan that God is using to build the highway. Without it we will endanger God's specific plans for us.

Peter had *"ears to hear."* Some of the disciples were murmuring over one of Christ's teaching (**"This is a hard teaching. Who can accept it?" John 6:60b**). After some thought about that *"hard teaching,"* **many of his disciples turned back and no longer followed him. John 6:66** Peter had a very different response to the same teaching. His response can be ours.

"You do not want to leave too, do you?" Jesus asked the Twelve. Simon Peter answered him, "Lord, to whom shall we go? You have the words of eternal life. We believe and know that you are the Holy One of God." John 6:67-69

If you are like me, you have a limit to the amount of information that you can *"hear"* in a day and respond to. I need some time to listen and some time to respond in each day. I may not like what I hear, but I must still respond. Managing my day so that I have both kinds of time is important.

Jesus said, *"consider carefully how you listen."* First I have to give him time. He wants to speak to me. Through the Bible, the Holy Spirit, and dozens of other ways He wants to speak to us. We must clear the way for Him to speak. Often we call the space we clear in our lives

31

for Him "quiet time." Quiet so we can have *"ears to hear."*

Once He has the opportunity to speak, then you need to *"consider carefully how you listen."* I read that Napoleon would wait three weeks after receiving his mail before he would open it. That way, most of it had already passed in importance and he didn't have to respond to it. He had an agenda for his life and he didn't want any interruptions. We need God's interruptions!

Christ's commands change every dimension of life. If we respond to what we hear from God we will *"be given more."* If our ears get wax in them and we cease to respond, *"even what he thinks he has will be taken from him."*

Showing God our love begins as we listen and obey. Giving money, singing loudly, or quoting words from the Bible doesn't mean a thing if we don't have *"ears to hear."* If we have heard but don't act on this new information, it can become out of date quickly. In fact *"even what he thinks he has will be taken from him."* Ears, listening, and obeying need to be a sequence that we make a part of our lives.

The master plan that God has for our lives will take a lot of instruction to complete. We must set aside time to hear, listen, and obey. When we do, we will be showing our love to God in the same way Jesus did; **"but the world must learn that I love the Father and that I do exactly what my Father has commanded me."** John 14:31a

Trouble and Fear

"Peace I leave with you; my peace I give you. I do not give to you as the world gives. Do not let your hearts be troubled and do not be afraid." John 14:27
Fully functional ears don't hear a thing when trouble and fear have paralyzed a heart. Opening our ears to hear from our Savior means we also have to make a commitment to keep the pathway to our hearts open.

We have some of the best roads in the country in my state. Good lighting, excellent signs, and on-going maintenance allows me to go wherever I need to go-most of the time.

Periodically, we have too much snow, rivers that want to use the roadway, trees that decide to lay down, and wind storms that carry our topsoil into the air in a blinding blanket. When these things happen, I can't get anywhere despite the quality of the roads.

We have the Bible in multiple translations; one to fit anyone's needs. You can get the Bible on tape and CD. There are more Christian books and ministries than ever before. Despite the quality, and quantity, that is available to us, troubled hearts and fearful souls won't benefit unless the ears to hear win out.

Jesus gave us peace to be our standard. When we don't have peace then it is a call to us to action. Something in the realm of trouble, fear, worry, anxiety, or stress has blocked the roadway from our ears to our hearts.

Only action on our part will clear the path; action that is consistent with the two white lines that Christ's commands paint.

Therefore, since we have a great high priest who has gone through the heavens, Jesus the Son of God, let us hold firmly to the faith we profess. For we do not have a high priest who is unable to sympathize with our weaknesses, but we have one who has been tempted in every way, just as we are—yet was without sin. Let us then approach the throne of grace with confidence, so that we may receive mercy and find grace to help us in our time of need. Hebrews 4:14-16

Jesus went out as usual to the Mount of Olives, and his disciples followed him. On reaching the place, he said to them, "Pray that you will not fall into temptation." He withdrew about a stone's throw beyond them, knelt down and prayed, "Father, if you are willing, take this cup from me; yet not my will, but yours be done." An angel from heaven appeared to him and strengthened him. And being in anguish, he prayed more earnestly, and his sweat was like drops of blood falling to the ground. Luke 22:39-44

We may never face death for our faith, but we might. Fear, trouble, anxiety, stress, and worry can come from any kind of experience that we are not comfortable with. An argument, a threat, confusion, uncertainty, anger, lies we hear, or a thousand other things can generate it. Like Jesus, we need to go to our Heavenly Father who sits on the throne in Heaven and get the help we need. We will need help to keep our ears open and not let the troubled heart win-get help!

During one particular period in my life I was ministering to three suicidal people. Dealing with that responsibility could have driven me to the same conclusions they had made: give up and end it all. Prayer made the difference for me. When I had lost the peace and panic was my first reaction, I would get on my knees and pray. During those times, I went to the throne and got the help I needed. With the peace I had ears to hear what I needed to do next.

We can *let* our hearts be troubled. We can *allow* fear to turn a noise from the refrigerator into an escaped convict in the bushes outside. Or we can go to the throne and get the peace that God offers. With His peace, our ears can hear the next step we are to take. Without the peace, panic can ruin a day and a lifetime.

We used a definition for panic when I was a lifeguard so we could properly deal with drowning people. Panic: the sudden unreasoning and overwhelming fear that attacks people in the face of real or fanciful danger. Real or fanciful danger was fatal. It produced an energy crisis. Abilities that could keep you alive now turned against you as panic robbed you of what strength you do have.

Jesus knows that definition too. Our ability to know Father God and go to Him in times of trouble allows us to live in peace. He also knew that if people did not understand, they were headed for the heartache and despair of panic. **"Those on the rock are the ones who receive the word with joy when they hear it, but they have no root. They believe for a while, but in the time of testing they fall away. The seed that fell among thorns stands for those who hear, but as they go on their way they are choked by *life's worries*** (italics are mine), **riches and pleasures, and they do not mature. "Luke 8:13-14**

Take My Yoke

"Come to me, all you who are weary and burdened, and I will give you rest. Take my yoke upon you and learn from me, for I am gentle and humble in heart, and you will find rest for your souls. For my yoke is easy and my burden is light." Matthew 11:28-30

In certain parts of the world you can still find animals out in the field burdened by a yoke and plow. But everywhere you go, you find people who are weary and burdened. Wearied by the yoke they carry and burdened by the pressures it brings.

Jesus could see it in people. So Jesus is offering a trade. Our mess for a life He gives to us and lives with us.

When we put on His yoke we agree to plow His field. Like any farmer who is dependent on his animals, He will take good care of us. He will work alongside us every minute of every day; He knows what our day is like. We will work just as hard as when we plowed our own field, but we aren't in charge anymore. That responsibility belongs to Jesus.

Jesus gives on-the-job-training, too. If you have never plowed before, He will show you how. You will learn how to deal with rocks and roots. He will show you the different strategies you need to pull in mud, clay, dust, and ground that has never been plowed before. He will be **"gentle"** in all this, though the task may be just the opposite.

When we pull His plow we will get to see His results. If we spend our energy on our own ideas, we get to see our results. **He who works *HIS*** (italics and capital letters are mine) **land will have abundant food, but the one who chases fantasies will have his fill of poverty. Proverbs 28:19**

If you are weary and burdened in your Christian life, it is time to stop and listen. Is this your creation, or did Jesus ask you to do it? If Jesus asked you to start this course of action, have you asked Him for any advice along the way? Are you trying to accomplish tomorrow's goals, today? Are you worrying about the issues that you are facing?

When we aren't rested in our soul, we need to talk to Jesus. We need to learn something from Him. He carried His Heavenly Father's yoke (the cross) and understands. When you pull His plow at His pace you accomplish His will and bless Him immeasurably. When you pull your plow at your pace you join the ranks of the weary and burdened. Long after you have given up, those carrying His yoke will see the harvest and know why they did what they did.

Each new season can bring a greater resolve and capacity to learn. That will allow for a greater harvest than the year before and a greater appreciation for the master of the field. **Let us not become weary in doing good, for at the proper time we will reap a harvest if we do not give up. Galatians 6:9**

His seed, His harvest

Jesus said to him, "Today salvation has come to this house, because this man, too, is a son of Abraham. For the Son of Man came to seek and save what was lost." Luke 19:9-10

Jesus came to find people who did not have a relationship with His Heavenly Father. When He found them, He would offer them that relationship.

That relationship required the space that repentance brings. If people did not repent then that person could have an experience with God, but no relationship. In the closeness of the relationship, what Jesus did became what the people (disciples) did. As they took the yoke that Jesus offered, they began to pave the property that repentance had cleared.

All of us will be asked to travel some distance to share the Gospel. It may only be across the street or it could be around the world. But all of us will need to learn how to share this Gospel message.

Salvation is found in no one else, for there is no other name under heaven given to men by which we must be saved. Acts 4:12 Jesus answered, "I am the way and the truth and the life. No one comes to the Father except through me. John 14:6

If you have experienced salvation and the privilege of going to the Father that Jesus provided for us, you have all the necessary knowledge to begin. There are many ways to share this good news Gospel. Some will preach, others will write, songs will be sung, quiet conversations will abound, and people will work as teams to spread this good news worldwide. If we don't participate in this area, we will find that our highway will have long stretches without pavement or paint. Until the whole world has heard and responded we have a job to do; it is the essence of the new life Jesus offered us.

The Lord is not slow in keeping his promise, as some understand slowness. He is patient with you, not wanting anyone to perish, but everyone to come to repentance. 2 Peter 3:9 "Come, follow me," Jesus said, "and I will make you fishers of men." Mark 1:17

Jesus sent the Holy Spirit to work with us after His return to Heaven. The Holy Spirit will counsel (John 16:7), convict (John 16:8), guide (John 16:13), teach, and remind (John 14:26). As he does this He will carry on the work in you that Jesus promised to His followers; *"Come, follow me, and I will make you fishers of men."*

Each of us needs to pay the price and learn about evangelism. We can care for people who don't have a relationship with God. We can plant God's seed to see God's harvest. We will try to obey, to be *"fishers of men."*

A variety of factors will determine the amount of harvest we will see in our lifetime. What specific talents did God give us? When did we hear the Gospel ourselves and respond? How much training did we get to equip us for the harvest work? Did we take advantage of the opportunities that were there for us in our circumstances? Do other issues distract us? Have these *"lost"* people ever heard this good news before or are we the first ones to share it with them?

How, then, can they call on the one they have not believed in? And how can they believe in the one of whom they have not heard? And how can they hear without someone preaching to them? Romans 10:14 "As you sent me into the world, I have sent them into the world." John 17:18

Learning to be a *"fisher of men"* will be the one constant definition of love that Christ's commands will paint for each of us. Loving God, will include loving people enough to learn how to share this good news with them.

Caught in the Act

One of the duties at an engineering job I had involved soil testing. It meant spending about six hours out in the middle of nowhere pouring water into a hole I had dug in the ground. One blue-sky day I noticed a huge cloud rising up over the tree line in the distance. It was not a day for clouds and this one was unique. "Jesus is coming back!" I was a new Christian but I had read that Jesus was coming back on a cloud at a time you would least expect Him. I wondered what to do. Should I run to the nearest house and try to tell them Jesus was coming? Should I jump to make it easier for Jesus? My heart was racing with excitement as I considered my options.

Then I remembered that Mt. St. Helen was still acting like a volcano and erupting. Sure enough, the cloud turned into a plume and I had to slow my heart down and get back to the business at hand.

Since that time I have heard many others tell stories from their own experience on this topic. Yet most of the time they were terrified at the prospect of Christ's return. Why two very different reactions? Some are ready for Christ's return, some aren't.

"Who then is the faithful and wise servant, whom the master has put in charge of the servants in his

household to give them their food at the proper time? It will be good for that servant whose master finds him doing so when he returns. I tell you the truth, he will put him in charge of all his possessions. But suppose that servant is wicked and says to himself, 'My master is staying away a long time,' and he then begins to beat his fellow servants and to eat and drink with drunkards. The master of that servant will come on a day when he does not expect him and at an hour he is not aware of. He will cut him to pieces and assign him a place with the hypocrites, where there will be weeping and gnashing of teeth." Matthew 24:45-51

Obedience to Christ's commands will open up a whole universe of experience that we can't have any other way. First, we find that we will be ready for the day He comes back. That will eliminate a lot of unnecessary worry and fear. Then as we obey His commands, we change. We start to become what we are doing (being "Christ-like"), even though initially it may be only out of obedience. Most importantly, we will begin to develop a very intimate relationship with our Lord. A relationship based on what He considers to be the most important work we can do.

"For whoever does the will of My Father in heaven, is my brother and sister and mother." Matthew 12:50 "You are my friends if you do what I command. I no longer call you servants, because a servant does not know his master's business. Instead, I have called you friends, for everything that I learned from my Father I have made known to you." John 15:14-15

As we obey, we enter into partnership with Jesus and the **"master's business."** Working with Him will produce an understanding of His heart and our purpose here on earth. It will also help us to prioritize our lives around what is important.

"Martha, Martha," the Lord answered, **"you are worried and upset about many things, but only one thing is needed. Mary has chosen what is better, and it will not be taken away from her." Luke 10:41-42**

Too often Jesus is appreciated as Savior but tolerated as Lord. That struggle is usually greatest when we don't see life in the same way Jesus does. This will happen if we haven't spent enough time with Him doing the master's business. That process of prioritizing will take place on a daily basis. So obedience is not a one-time choice. It takes place every day for the rest of our life.

Then he said to them all, "If anyone would come after me, he must deny himself and take up his cross daily and follow me." Luke 9:23

Jesus forgave us of our entire past; let's give Him our entire future. If we live that way, we don't have to fear His return; we will get caught in the act of obedience.

When You Pray

Prayer needs a good definition. Depending on where you are and whom you talk to, it can mean almost anything. In some groups it means spinning a prayer wheel. Their prayers have been written down on a cylinder and it is spun. Each time the wheel goes around, the prayer goes up. So by spinning these cylinders rapidly, you can pray a lot. For another group, prayer must take place at certain times of the day facing in a certain direction where memorized prayers are repeated. Travel in another direction and you find people standing on street corners praying loudly.

Jesus understands the confusion so He gave us some guidelines that help us know how to pray and, more importantly, understand the heart of prayer. Looking at Matthew 6:5-15 we will get a good start on prayer.

"When you pray." Matthew 6:5a Our first guideline tells us to pray. As you read through the New Testament you will see that Jesus prayed a lot. Sometimes it was at night or early morning. Prayer preceded big decisions and events. Eventually the disciples recognized that Jesus' unique prayer life and His miraculous ministry were linked together. So they asked Him to teach them how to pray.

After Jesus had gone back to Heaven, you find the disciples have learned this lesson on prayer; now they pray a lot. Interestingly enough, their new prayer life produces the same miracle-filled ministry that Jesus had. Miracles are not the point of prayer but they are a by-product of the kind of prayer Jesus taught. Learn to pray following the guidelines that Jesus gave.

"But when you pray, go into your room, close the door and pray to your Father." Matthew 6:6a Privacy, not secrecy, is the second guideline for prayer. Prayer is a conversation between you and Father God. You need the privacy because you need to hear Him and He wants to talk to you. There will be times for public prayer. When you are praying for the sick or the needs of people in a group, you will pray publicly. But for your own life and relationship with Father God, you need to pray in private. Then He can say whatever needs to be said and you can respond honestly and openly.

We also get to pray to Father God. Jesus opened the door to Him for us. Jesus' sacrifice enables us to enter into the throne room of Father God and present our needs, concerns, confusion, and questions and leave with all the wisdom, mercy and grace that we need for what lies ahead.

Let us then approach the throne of grace with confidence, so that we may receive mercy and find grace to help us in our time of need. Hebrews 4:16 If any of you lacks wisdom, he should ask God, who gives generously to all without finding fault, and it will be given to him. James 1:5 For you did not receive a spirit that makes you a slave again to fear, but you received the Spirit of sonship. And by him we cry, *"Abba, Father."* The Spirit himself testifies with our spirit that we are God's children. Romans 8:15-16

Entering into the presence of Father God is an essential element of prayer. Christ's sacrifice is so complete that we can meet Father God face to face, without fear. If you have confessed all sin then you are free to go in. All the teachings on prayer in the New Testament assume that we are praying from this posture.

Too often we come as beggars, or our heads hung in shame, or unsure that we will have an audience with Father God. At those times, it's like praying through a peephole in the door. We can't see what's going on. We are talking to an unknown. My own kids only talk to me that way when they are in trouble. Because of Jesus, we can deal with our sin whenever it happens. We don't have to be in trouble anymore.

Next to our own guilt and shame, we will have to deal with the thought factory in our minds. In order to experience the presence of Father God, we need to be able to focus our attention on the conversation. I have had many conversations with people where it was obvious that they were thinking about something else. Communication never takes place when only one side of the relationship is there. When you pray, you will have Father God's full attention; will He have yours?

You can see why Jesus told us not to worry. Worry can rob us of our time in Father God's presence. Ironically, He is the only one who could help us on whatever it is that is consuming us.

"And when you pray, do not keep on babbling like pagans, for they think they will be heard because of their many words. Do not be like them, for your Father knows what you need before you ask him." Matthew 6:7-8

In the presence of Father God, you can have a conversation with Him. If you try to use volumes of words to make your point, it is really an insult to the relationship that you have with Him. Say it with all your heart; but if you're in His presence, know that He heard it. If you give

Him time, you will have a peace in your heart that confirms to you that He heard it.

I hope you can see that the Bible is describing prayer as more than a five-minute a day exercise. It is a conversation with the Creator of the Universe. You will need to rearrange your day and life to make time for this privilege. As you do, you will begin to hear His voice on a regular basis. In time, it will be the radio that keeps you informed as you travel down the highway that repentance cleared and obedience paved.

How You Pray

"This, then, is how you should pray:

"'Our Father in heaven,
hallowed be your name,
your kingdom come,
your will be done
on earth as it is in heaven.
Give us today our daily bread.
Forgive us our debts,
as we also have forgiven our debtors.
And lead us not into temptation,
but deliver us from the evil one.'"
Matthew 6:9-13

We have a relationship with the Creator of the Universe that is so intimate and secure that we can call Him **"Father."** Just the word **"Father"** will at some point bring tears to your eyes and overwhelm you. Overwhelm you with the privilege that Jesus has made possible for us. Even if it is a hard word for you to use, don't stop. In time its full meaning will become real for you, if you don't close the door to it.

"**Father**" also denotes our position. There is someone above us who has a very influential role in our lives if we allow Him. If He is "**Father,**" then we are sons or daughters. Keeping that perspective is very important as we grow in our roles and responsibilities in life. No matter how important or respected we are by people, we still need to consult our "**Father**" before we make our decisions.

To keep our intimate and secure relationship from becoming casual or neglected, we are reminded that He is "**in heaven**" and "**hallowed.**" It is easy to become indifferent to something or someone whom we see on a regular basis. Marriages fall apart all the time because someone was taken for granted. God's place and position won't allow that, if we enter His presence. We can utter words in God's direction at a meal or before we rush off to another activity, but we dare not call that prayer. When we enter into His presence, we will know that He is in heaven and that His name is to be hallowed (respected as holy). He will expose any sin in our lives and speak clearly to us about any needed direction or correction for our lives.

Once we are in His presence, we realize that He has an agenda for our lives and this world. He has plans. Heaven is a place of incredible activity. We are a part of fulfilling those plans. He wants us to have hearts that cooperate as we speak, "**your kingdom come, your will be done on earth as it is in heaven.**"

His words become your heart's desire as you travel down this new highway His ways have built. If you ever find yourselves running out of gas, check your motivation. If it isn't based on His will then He won't refuel you. In fact, He will work on changing the way you spend your time.

Knowing what the Bible says will help us a lot in this area of doing God's will. Any basic command in scripture is God's will for everyone. Those found in this book would fit that description. Specific commands ("be a missionary in Brazil") would have to come from God Himself.

"Give us today our daily bread." It has been years since I have had to look for pennies hoping to find enough money for a loaf of bread. That could all change in a matter of weeks if our economy failed. Then I would be like the rest of the world where food is a very relevant need. Until that happens, I still need to be thankful that He has so blessed my nation that I not only have my daily bread but have a choice of white, wheat, sour dough, raisin, rye, and pumpernickel.

"Forgive" is the word that makes prayer possible. Father God will forgive us for any sin that we will honestly confess to Him. He also expects us to **"have forgiven our debtors."** His example towards us becomes a command for us to others.

"For if you forgive men when they sin against you, your heavenly Father will also forgive you. But if you do not forgive men their sins, your Father will not forgive your sins." Matthew 6:14-15

"And lead us not into temptation, but deliver us from the evil one." As we pray, that is possible. If we don't pray, that becomes impossible. If we follow, He will not lead us into temptation. Our time in prayer will allow Father God to correct our direction, speed, and destination. That correction will keep us from falling into the traps that **"temptation"** brings.

When we pray in a day isn't critical; *that* we pray every day is. *How* we pray will determine if we really pray. For myself, I have a simple definition of prayer. Pray until I'm different and Father God is done. Sometimes that can mean twenty minutes. Other times it is hours. Often I end up with a fresh "To Do List." I have learned that what is started in my first prayer of the day doesn't have to stop. I can continue to praise Him, thank Him, ask Him, and hear from Him throughout the day. **Be joyful always; pray continually; give thanks in all circumstances, for this is God's will for you in Christ Jesus. 1 Thessalonians 5:16-18**

Because You Pray

"Have faith in God, "Jesus answered. "I tell you the truth, if anyone says to this mountain, 'Go throw yourself into the sea, and does not doubt in his heart but believes that what he says will happen, it will be done for him. Therefore I tell you, whatever you ask for in prayer believe that you have received it, and it will be yours." Mark 11:22-24

"Have faith in God," and get your faith from Him. As we spend our time in prayer and pray for **"your will to be done,"** He will give us His desires that can become our prayers.

Years ago we needed our first computer and did not have the income to afford one. As I was praying, I sensed that I could ask for a computer from Father God; so I did. We started to save all the extra money that came to us and within six weeks we had a computer and printer. My faith to ask came from time in His presence. Faith comes from our face-to-face time with Father God.

If the request is only dependent on us and Father God then the process can be simple. We have the faith to ask and believe based on our face-to-face time with Father God. Father God answers the prayer. If others are involved then there are additional factors that can determine the outcome.

But Jesus said to them, "Only in his hometown and in his own house is a prophet without honor." And he did not do many miracles there because of their lack of faith. Matthew 13:57-58

When you pray for others, you are walking into a whole new realm of faith and answered prayer. They may not have any faith; you won't be able to see many miracles.

If you don't get the real cause of the problem, your prayer may not have any effect at all. Praying for a financial miracle for someone may not be answered, based on how they are handling their finances. So praying for others requires the same faith that comes from a face-to-face contact with Father God.

My kids ask me for many things. And they usually know the answer before I give it. Some things they ask for they know will get a "yes." Others they know will get a "no" but they ask anyway. Those in the "maybe" range are the ones that have the mystery about them. What will dad say? When we know Father God and His views, we will be able to have the same kind of anticipation with Him.

If we are approaching Father God with some inappropriate requests or ones based on incomplete information then that time in His presence will help us to see that. Conversely, if we aren't sure about a request before we ask Him, we can become very confident as we enter His presence and find that He is also desirous of that same thing.

You can see that this kind of prayer is time consuming. But this kind of prayer, based on how you should pray, enables you to see results. Praying this way will also allow Father God to reveal Himself to you.

Faith produces another aspect of the Christian life: vision. Vision is Father God's specific direction and purpose for your life and those you are responsible for. If Father God has called you to preach to the world, He will cultivate that thought and heart in you while you are in His presence. If that isn't in His plan for you then He won't encourage you in it.

His vision becomes your vision in His presence. Then you can get your vision revised and updated in His presence as often as it becomes the topic of discussion with Him.

Faith can be misunderstood if it is defined any other way. When that happens people build their beliefs on shaky ground. Instead we are called to build on a rock; the rock of Christ's teachings that include when, how, and because we pray.

When You Fast

"**They will fast,**" is found in **Matthew 9:15, Mark 2:20, and Luke 5:35** While Jesus walked the earth people asked Him why His disciples did not fast. He replied that "**they will fast**" after they came to a point where they understood fasting. Fasting was a common part of the religious life of that time. But it was only a religious exercise. The purpose of fasting had been lost in the regulated public practice that it had become.

"**No one sews a patch of un-shrunk cloth on an old garment, for the patch will pull away from the garment, making the tear worse. Neither do men pour new wine into old wineskins. If they do, the skins will burst, the wine will run out and the wineskins will be ruined. No, they pour new wine into new wineskins, and both are preserved.**" Matthew 9:16-17.

"**When you fast,**" **(Matthew 6:16a)** was looking forward to the time when the disciples understood fasting and Jesus was back in heaven. When those two conditions were met, the disciples fasted (Acts 13 & 14 are examples).

Understanding the true heart of fasting requires a look back to the Old Testament and forward to the New Testament. In these examples we can find the purpose in fasting that Jesus' disciples would soon understand.

Since we live by the Spirit, let us keep in step with the Spirit. Galatians 5:25 **Those who live according to the sinful nature have their minds set on what that nature desires; but those who live in accordance with the Spirit have their minds set on what the Spirit desires.** Romans 8:5 **Dear friends, I urge you, as aliens and strangers in the world, to abstain from sinful desires, which war against your soul.** 1 Peter 2:11

There is a war between our desire to do what the Holy Spirit is saying and what our human desires are. The Spirit says, "get up at 5 am." The human desire says, "6:30 am will do." The Spirit says, "tell that stranger about Jesus." The human desire says, "they won't listen to you, don't waste your time." When you fast, you have a capacity to focus on the Spirit's desires as you say "no" to the human desire to eat.

When radios were tuned by turning a dial you could have your radio tuned exactly where you wanted it, but you would have to periodically adjust it anyway to keep the desired station. Your radio dial had not been moved; none the less, the station became fuzzy. In our efforts to follow Jesus we need to periodically focus once again on the Spirit's voice. A fast forces that. You don't have unlimited energy **"when you fast."** You can't keep a hectic schedule. Your body slows down. It is difficult to be proud or arrogant when you don't have the energy to maintain that attitude. You are in a position to be changed. After you learn that you won't starve to death (something your body will try to tell you), you can settle down and the Spirit will have time to readjust your dial.

Moses received the ten commandments while fasting (Exodus 34:28). Daniel needed to hear from Father God and he prepared himself by fasting (Daniel 9). Jesus fought the desires of the human nature and the advice of the Devil while fasting (Matthew 4). As these people focused with a fast they were **"in step with the Spirit"** and knew His desires and the power to accomplish them.

This kind of fasting can be a planned part of your life. You can put it on a calendar and protect those days, so they aren't lost to other activities. At other times, being able to plan life is only a dream so you will need to deal with some unplanned realities as well.

My heart is blighted and withered like grass; I forget to eat my food. Psalm 102:4 Fasting can also be a partner with times of intense emotion and stress. The prophet Joel called the people to fast because they were at a critical point in the history of their nation, **"Even now," declares the Lord, "return to me with all your heart, with fasting and weeping and mourning." Rend your heart and not your garments. Return to the Lord your God, for he is gracious and compassionate, slow to anger and abounding in love, and he relents from sending calamity." Joel 2:12-13**

David fasted for his son who was dying (2 Samuel 12:16-20). Esther fasted before she approached the king with a life-threatening situation (Esther 4:15-16). Ezra fasted when he realized the full sin of his nation (Ezra 10). The focus of fasting allows you to bear the next step you must take. It is an honest expression of the intensity of the moment. You can't plan for these kinds of situations, but you can respond to them with fasting.

Planned and responsive fasting each have their place. Ritualistic fasting doesn't. That was one of the problems Jesus was facing when He walked this earth. It wasn't a new problem in Israel.

The people of Bethel had sent Sharezer and Regem-Melech, together with their men, to entreat the Lord by asking the priests of the house of the Lord Almighty and the prophets, "Should I mourn and fast in the fifth month, as I have done for so many years?"

Then the word of the Lord Almighty came to me: "Ask all the people of the land and the priests, 'When you fasted and mourned in the fifth and seventh months for the past seventy years, was it really for me that you fasted?'" **Zechariah 7:2-5**

"When you fast," do so out of obedience to the prompting of the Holy Spirit and the needs at hand. As you learn to do that, you will see the reasons behind Jesus' response, **"then they will fast."**

How You Fast

"When you fast, do not look somber as the hypocrites do, for they disfigure their faces to show men they are fasting. I tell you the truth, they have received their reward in full. But when you fast, put oil on your head and wash your face, so that it will not be obvious to men that you are fasting, but only to your Father who is unseen; and your Father, who sees what is done in secret, will reward you. Matthew 6:16-18

How you fast is just as important as the fact that you are fasting. When the religious people of Jesus' day fasted, you knew it (it was a public event) and were impressed at their dedication and sacrifice. You were impressed but Father God wasn't.

Religion had become a political platform, not a relationship platform. The Jewish religious leaders were more concerned with the power and place (John 11:48) they held politically than their role in knowing God. Fasting helped reinforce the political position; not a relationship role with God. So Jesus had to tell His disciples what not to do just as much as He had to tell them what to do.

So don't go un-shaven, un-showered, and un-kempt. If you do, people will have to ask you why; and you will have to tell them. Then you have lost the focus of fasting; your relationship with Father God.

How you fast can have at least four general categories with unlimited variations. You can abstain totally from any kind of food or liquid; that would be a total fast (Moses, Exodus 34:28). This is a supernatural fast, so you better have Father God write it on the wall for you.

You can also abstain from food and just drink water (Jesus, Matthew 4:2, "thirst isn't mentioned"); that would be a food fast. Other times you could fast from certain types of food or beverages. Daniel abstained from **"choice food: no meat or wine." Daniel 10:3a**

There is also a scriptural fast described in Isaiah 58 where you eat normally but your activities change. What kind of fast you are going to do will depend on the time you are fasting and why Father God is calling you to fast.

I can't give you any advice or teaching on a total supernatural fast. IF Father God called you to that, it would all have to be a supernatural call and provision. He did not design our bodies to function that way. Normally we start to have some serious physical complications if we don't get fluids after three days.

For a food fast you will have to recognize the fact that you won't have the energy, stamina, or endurance that you normally have. That is a part of the design. You will slow down and focus all that you are on your Heavenly Father. Planning that into your calendar is important. For example, if you are going to fast for three days, you could eat your last meal Thursday night. Go to work and get hungry but then have Saturday and Sunday where you can control your time and activity better. Don't plan on building a deck that weekend. Not only would you have some potential problems, but you also would have forfeited the reason why you were fasting in the first place: focus.

If you are fasting because of a crisis or need, you would center all your focus time on intercession. If it is a fast to focus, you ought to have extended periods of prayer, Bible reading, and study. You also need to rest when you feel that you are exhausted. A fast will focus you spiritually, but it can also be a time of great physical refreshing as well. Slowing down your pace may be just what you need physically.

Partial fasts will allow you to continue to work or do projects for Jesus. Abstaining from certain kinds of foods or beverages can help you in the battle that always exists between the human part of you and the supernatural Holy Spirit. Sweets and caffeine are two modern-day substitutes (Ephesians 5:18-20) for the energy and vitality that the Holy Spirit can provide. Fasting from them will show you just what is chemically induced in your life and what is from the Holy Spirit. When you see that in a fast, it may be a signal that you need to make some lifestyle changes to live within the boundaries our Father in Heaven has designed into you. Changes that will help you to be **"in step with the Spirit." Galatians 5:25b.**

"Is not this the kind of fasting I have chosen: to loose the chains of injustice and untie the cords of the yoke, to set the oppressed free and break every yoke? Is it not to share your food with the hungry and to provide the poor wanderer with shelter—when you see the naked, to clothe him, and not to turn away from your own flesh and blood? Isaiah 58:6-7

Fasting is a command from Jesus. The focus it brings can't be attained any other way. The things you learn about yourself can't be learned any other way, either.

It can be a meal you skip or a day or longer. Don't be afraid of it; and at the same time be ready to struggle with it. Your human nature will ALWAYS want to eat unless you are under stress. So work out the times when you fast with Father God.

Because You Fast

"And your Father, who sees what is done in secret, will reward you." Matthew 6:18b With the focus of fasting comes a reward. As you scan the Old and New Testaments you will find the kinds of rewards that Father God gave and still gives today.

While they were worshipping the Lord and fasting, the Holy Spirit said, "Set apart for me Barnabas and Saul for the work to which I have called them" Acts 13:2 Barnabas and Saul received clear direction for their lives. It was also made known to the whole church so that they could support and pray for them. This is one of the most practical rewards of fasting. As you focus, Father God's plans become clearer. Were those thoughts and ideas God's or mine? Time in His focused presence will determine that; He will build on them, modify them, or dismiss them altogether.

Now faith is being sure of what we hope for and certain of what we do not see. Hebrews 11:1 Our faith will grow as we spend that focused time with Him. For me, He always works out some new kind of ministry breakthrough while I am fasting. People have gotten saved, delivered, and healed. Other times, new opportunities to minister come to me during those times. I have sometimes wondered what my life would be like if I always fasted (besides short). This tie between my fasting, my focus, and His action builds my faith to new levels every time.

Even youths grow tired and weary, and young men stumble and fall; but those who *hope* (italics mine) **in the Lord will renew their strength. They will soar on wings like eagles; they will run and not grow weary, they will walk and not be faint. Isaiah 40:30-31** The word *hope* means an "intertwining." If you were a thin, old, cheap, kite string, you would not expect to have a very useful existence. You would know that your capacity would be limited to a party balloon or some string art. But if you could intertwine yourself with a two-inch dock rope, you could do anything that rope could do. So it is when we are refreshed by those times of fasting with Father God. We become intertwined, refreshed, and ready to soar.

You do not delight in sacrifice, or I would bring it; you do not take pleasure in burnt offerings. The sacrifices of God are a broken spirit; a broken and contrite heart, O God, you will not despise. Psalm 51:16-17 When you take away the energy and activity that food brings, you are left with yourself and the Holy Spirit of God. At those times, He speaks to you. Your focus allows Him that privilege. If needed, He will speak words of correction, conviction, or comfort. All those break our hearts so He can rebuild them again. That repaired and renewed heart motivates us down the highway much farther and faster than the old one could.

When Ahab heard these words, he tore his clothes, put on sackcloth and fasted. He lay in sackcloth and went around meekly. Then the word of the Lord came to Elijah the Tishbite: "Have you noticed how Ahab has humbled himself before me? Because he has humbled himself, I will not bring this disaster in his

day, but I will bring it on his house in the days of his son." 1 Kings 21:27-29

One of the most wicked kings in Israel's existence was able to change history when he focused on God with a proper fast. What He will do with you, through you, and for you is hard to tell. Fasting does not turn your desires into your future. But it does make possible His desires that involve you. Father God's desire for King Ahab was a change of heart and a submission to His ways. The king responded. We can, too.

When I heard these things, I sat down and wept. For some days I mourned and fasted and prayed before the God of heaven. Nehemiah 1:4 The king said to me, "What is it you want?" Then I prayed to the God of heaven, and I answered the king, "If it pleases the king and if your servant has found favor in his sight, let him send me to the city in Judah where my fathers are buried so that I can rebuild it." Then the king, with the queen sitting beside him, asked me, "How long will your journey take, and when will you get back?" It pleased the king to send me; so I set a time. Nehemiah 2:4-6

Nehemiah became aware of a problem. It broke his heart, so he fasted and prayed. Within days he was able to be a part of the solution to the problem that had broken his heart just days before. When we face problems that don't seem to have a solution, we need that face-to-face time with God and the favor that He alone can grant us with others.

When Jesus saw that a crowd was running to the scene, he rebuked the evil spirit. "You deaf and mute spirit," he said, "I command you, come out of him and never enter him again." The spirit shrieked, convulsed him violently and came out. The boy looked so much like a corpse that many said, "He's dead." But Jesus

took him by the hand and lifted him to his feet, and he stood up. After Jesus had gone indoors, his disciples asked him privately, "Why couldn't we drive it out?" He replied, "This kind can come out only by prayer (some versions *"and fasting"*). Mark 9:25-29

As you spend that focused time with Father God, you often become more aware of and capable in the use of the ministry gifts of the Holy Spirit (1 Corinthians 12:7-11, 27-31). Some of these gifts are given to us at our salvation. Others are given at our request. And still others are given to us in times of need. The disciples had encountered something they couldn't overcome. Jesus showed them that it could be overcome with the added focus that prayer and fasting can bring.

Fasting is not the fast track to Father God or a cure for the hassles of life. It is a way to get down to the real basic issues of life and deal with them. **"When you fast,"** remember Christ's words and you will see His results.

When You Give

Money can represent social status, achievement, opportunity, values, and power. These possibilities make it a critical issue in life. Jesus addressed the money issues on a regular basis because He knew the impact that money can have in a person's life. If we learn from His commands in this area, we will be a strong viable part in the body of Christ. If we don't, we will drag a lot of heartache and hassle into His church.

"No one can serve two masters. Either he will hate the one and love the other, or he will be devoted to the one and despise the other. You cannot serve both God and Money." Matthew 6:24 The place that Father God should have in someone's life can be lost to money. As it is in all counterfeits, the person who accepts it gets burned. If you accept counterfeit money, no one refunds you the real thing when you find out, not even a bank. You've been burned. When you accept money as your master, you've been burned, and will burn forever in Hell if you don't realize this counterfeit soon enough.

Money is supposed to be a classroom subject. God uses it to teach us principles that impact our entire lives. Unfortunately, people see the power that money represents and they don't learn the lessons that they need for life.

Instead, they try to use money to solve the problems they face rather than use the commands Christ left for us. Generosity, trust, faith, and sacrifice are just a few of the lessons you can learn through money. You can also flunk all of those lessons if you hold on to the money too tightly. You need to learn about an exchange program instead.

When you travel, you learn how to exchange money so it has value in your new country. In God's kingdom, you have the opportunity to exchange the money you have earned and turn it into ministry. Giving to workers and programs allows you to make a difference in countries and situations that you will never see yourself.

We can exchange the money we earn for something of value in the Kingdom of God. Giving is one of the ways we will do that. There is one basic giving guideline and four basic giving areas.

"So when you give to the *needy.*" Matthew 6:2a John answered, "*The man with two* tunics should share with him who has none, and the one who has food should do the same." Luke 3:11 Since Judas had charge of the money, some thought Jesus was telling him to buy what was *needed* for the Feast, or to give something to the poor. John 13:29 All the believers were together and had everything in common. *Selling their possessions and goods, they gave* to anyone as he had *need.* Acts 2:44-45 *If anyone has* material possessions and sees his brother in *need* but has no pity on him, how can the love of God be in him? 1 John 3:17 (Italics mine)

Give to those in need when you have an abundance. That is the basic guideline. Two things immediately shout, "define that for me; need and abundance."

In Bible times, people were often in need because there was no such thing as job security, Visa cards, sick pay, welfare, or insurance. The lady of the house didn't have refrigeration or canning so she had to shop on a daily basis. All these conditions meant that a person's personal economy was fairly volatile. Bad weather, poor crops, disease, or national politics could wipe you out fairly quickly.

Today in our country we have many safety nets that catch us before we hit the realm of need. That doesn't mean we won't get to that point, but it isn't as easy. However, much of the rest of the world still lives on the same basic level as those described in Bible times. That is why tens of thousands of people starve to death every day worldwide. They aren't lazy people; they just live in a volatile economy.

Giving to those in need for the basics is one definition of need. That one area takes on two aspects: needs within the body of Christ and needs outside of the body of Christ. In scripture you don't find a distinction between the two. Practically speaking, we will react differently. It is easier to obey Christ's command to give to the needy when you know them from church. It is tougher to give to someone when they smell of alcohol and cigarettes. It is easier to give to a missionary preaching in your church about work among the poor than it is to respond to a mailing that everyone gets.

That is why we still need to pray about how much to give and how to give. It is easy not to give or to give sparingly when we don't have a personal attachment to the people or situation. You see, when you give to people in the church you are investing in the body of Christ. When you give to people outside the church, you are planting and watering the soil so that the seed of the Gospel will have a better chance. In either case, if you sow sparingly you will also reap sparingly (2 Corinthians 9:6-11).

We need to look at the idea of abundance (he who has two), as well to give a perspective to the scripture for our day and age. Paul took up a number of offerings to meet the needs of the Christians that he encountered as he traveled. This was his guiding principle as he talked to people about the needs and the opportunities to give: **Our desire is not that others might be relieved while you are hard pressed, but that there might be equality. At the present time your plenty will supply what they need, so that in turn their plenty will supply what you need. Then there will be equality, as it is written: "He who gathered much did not have too much, and he who gathered little did not have too little." 2 Corinthians 8:13-15**

Paul wanted people to give when they could and be able to ask when they had need. He saw the worldwide body of Christ meeting all its own needs. The resources could flow from an area of abundance to an area of need at any given time. With the redistribution there would be "equality" and the body would function without long term needs.

In making a transition from a cash society to a credit society, we have lost the simplicity of the Bible times in this area. What is something we can give away and what are real needs?

When you buy everything with cash, it is a lot easier to determine what is an abundance; you have it or you don't. With a credit society, you have bills and debts that are floating around on a payment basis. In one respect you could apply every penny you get to your debts. On the other hand, as long as you make your payments, you could give away what is left over. The problem in a debt story comes if you have a change in your income flow and you can no longer make your payments. Then you face financial penalties and the potential of losing everything you have to fulfill your debt obligations.

It also means that you may have two of something but you can't give one away because you owe money on both of them. Whoever you gave it to would have to make payments on it or trust that you would be able to make payments on it while they used it.

A credit society allows people to live life at a higher economic level than they can honestly afford. That means that the abundance factor is hard to measure. Yes, our country has a higher per capita income than it has ever had before. It also has the highest per capita debt as well. We have taken our new income levels and used them to finance our lifestyle with credit. That gets us to a higher level faster but puts our whole economic world in jeopardy.

What *is* our abundance? Complicated isn't it? Each individual will have to wrestle with this. How this works out ultimately will depend on how we apply another Biblical directive to our lives: contentment.

Keep your lives free from the love of money and be content with what you have, because God has said, "Never will I leave you; never will I forsake you." Hebrews 13:5

If we are content with what we have, we will have more to give away. The capacity to be content will be dependent on our level of trust and faith in God. If we trust Him to provide the needs and can listen to His personal guidance for us, we will have a pretty good understanding of what we can and should give. If we think we have to provide for all of our needs from the money that we earn and we aren't sure when God is directing us to give then, based on our level of insecurity, we will tend to hoard what finances we do have and pursue more.

Now we need to look at the third area of giving: people in ministry. From the time Jesus began to preach until his crucifixion, he was supported by offerings (Mark 15:41, John 12:4-6). Paul presented a powerful scriptural case **(1 Corinthians 9:1-14)** showing that **"those who preach the gospel should receive their living from the gospel."** It is a basic reality. You can get more done if you have more time.

Many preachers of the gospel work because the example of Christ and the command that Paul gave isn't obeyed in all places and under all conditions. Those that do preach will often face some kind of economic hardship, which can limit their effectiveness.

Because of the many media formats that we have (phone, mail, television, internet, etc.), we are aware of ministry needs around the world. We are also aware that some of the needs presented may not be valid. Scandals occur wherever there is money. The church world is no exception. We know that and are suspicious.

Despite that, ministries will not survive or thrive without the giving of the body of Christ. People in ministry will have a constant need for the ministry of giving. Who you give to can be a wrestling match sometimes. Tithes go to the local church (Malachi 3:6-12) but what about all the rest? You will have to wrestle with that one yourself.

Our final area may take more wrestling than all the rest. **"You have heard that it was said, 'Eye for eye, and tooth for tooth.' But I tell you, Do not resist an evil person. If some one strikes you on the right cheek, turn to him the other also. And if someone wants to sue you and take your tunic, let him have your cloak as well. If someone forces you to go one mile, go with him two miles. Give to the one who asks you, and do not turn away from the one who wants to borrow from you." Matthew 5:38-42**

There are more "evil" people all the time. You can be quite sure that when you give to them, you won't get it back. Sometimes they ask with guns in their hands. Giving to them is the first step in showing them the love (Matthew 5:43-48) that Christ showed towards those who hated Him. That demonstration of love prepared the hearts of those "evil" people to repent and turn in the weeks ahead at the preaching of Peter (Acts 14:14-41).

You are not showing weakness when you give to an "evil" person; you are saying that they are more valuable than the things you have. When you resist an "evil" person you are saying that your things are more valuable than they are; a message they have probably already heard.

"When you give," you will face many decisions. You have the basic guideline of giving out of your abundance to those in need. The needy will come from those in the church, outside the church, and those in ministry. Evil people will cross your path as well. You will have to wrestle on a regular basis with the implications of this command. Don't stop wrestling with this issue. That is the only way you will be able to maintain your devotion to God and your mastery over one of His chief competitors: money.

How You Give

"So when you give to the needy, do not announce it with trumpets, as the hypocrites do in the synagogues and on the streets, to be honored by men. I tell you the truth, they have received their reward in full. But when you give to the needy, do not let your left hand know what your right hand is doing, so that your giving may be in secret. Then your Father, who sees what is done in secret, will reward you." Matthew 6:2-4

Ever patted yourself on the back for a job well done? That won't happen if the other hand doesn't know what the first hand has given. Jesus lived in a culture where religious practices brought some of the highest praise from people. So those who wanted to look good made their donations public events. Everyone knew.

We do the same thing today. If we give, we get a brick with our name on it, a place on the plaque, or an invitation to a special donor's dinner, not to mention a tax credit.

"Secretly"-few know. One of the goals of all of Christ's commands is that we live our lives for and before our Heavenly Father. If we do our giving secretly, only Father God has the privilege of examining our motives and praising us. People seem to rise to the highest standard they are given.   Christ's standard will bring about a Christian lifestyle. If we lower ourselves to the standard of our culture, we will live a culturally consistent lifestyle. Give secretly.

And now, brothers, we want you to know about the grace that God has given the Macedonian churches. Out of the most severe trial, their overflowing joy and their extreme poverty welled up in rich generosity.   For I testify that they gave as much as they were able, and even beyond their ability.   Entirely on their own, they urgently pleaded with us for the privilege of sharing in this service to the saints. 2 Corinthians 8:1-4

They gave "generously" in the material world out of an "abundance" of joy in their hearts. Generosity means more than enough. It means that both the giver and receiver can feel good about what just took place. Paul was impressed with these people not because of how much they gave but because he knew how much they really had.

You can give five pennies or you can give a million dollars to a need. Both of those gifts could be generous or both could be given grudgingly.   When we have God's abundance in our heart the amount isn't the issue; the attitude is.

Each man should give what he has decided in his heart to give, not reluctantly or under compulsion, for God loves a cheerful giver. 2 Corinthians 9:7

You will be bombarded with requests for finances. How you give to each one will take some deciding.   Take the time to decide.   I take requests and either respond immediately or let them set for a while. If they get bigger and better in my heart while they are waiting, I will happily give out of my abundance. If there is no abundance to give from, I may give in some other way, like time in prayer.

Your heart can be a great place to make decisions as long as you allow the daily presence of Jesus to clear the air on all issues. Giving in a "get" happy land will never be easy. Like all areas of our growth and maturity in the commands of Christ, there will be struggles. Don't fear them; learn from Him for each one of them.

Not only so, but we also rejoice in our sufferings, because we know that suffering produces perseverance; perseverance, character; and character, hope. And hope does not disappoint us, because God has poured out his love into our hearts by the Holy Spirit, whom he has given us. Romans 5:3-5

In secret, give that generous gift out of the abundance, which only the love of God can make in a heart. Your cheerful way will be a blessing to everyone around you and your Father in Heaven will reward you.

Because You Give

Israel was given a great system to maintain what God had begun with that nation. God set apart the whole Levite tribe to serve the people by serving Him. Their job was to be godly. The other tribes of Israel were to support the Levites. These Levites were then to support the priests, the descendants of Aaron.

"I give to the Levites all the tithes in Israel as their inheritance in return for the work they do while serving at the Tent of Meeting. Numbers 18:21 They will receive no inheritance among the Israelites. Instead, I give to the Levites as their inheritance the tithes that the Israelites present as an offering to the Lord. Numbers 18:23b-24 The Lord said to Moses, "Speak to the Levites and say to them: 'When you receive from the Israelites the tithe I give you as your inheritance, you must present a tenth of that tithe as the Lord's offering.'" Numbers 18:25-26 From these tithes you must give the Lord's portion to Aaron the priest. Numbers 18:28b

When the people did this, it worked well. There was enough for everyone and the Levites and priests did their part in maintaining the godliness of that nation. When the people stopped giving their tithe (and they would) then the

Levites had to learn trades and spend their time like everyone else. That changed everything. The lack of funds contributed to the loss of focus of the nation. That loss of focus guaranteed a loss of godliness and the demise of the country.

By the time of Christ, rabbis (the new religious leaders of the new system) were taught a trade because everyone knew the original system wasn't working in Israel. This new system was full of corruption, pride, and religious leaders that didn't know the God they represented.

Tithing was God's original plan. By it, ten people can support one. Twenty people can support a pastor and the expenses of a small church. Thirty people can support the pastor, church, and a missionary. As you can see, the possibilities are exciting.

Unfortunately, in the USA less than 30% of the people who attend churches tithe. That means that you have more people to take care of and fewer finances to make it happen. That's one reason why churches have a reputation of always asking for money; everyone wants an exciting place to go to church but less than half are willing to obey God to pay for it.

Welcome him in the Lord with great joy, and honor men like him, because he almost died for the work of Christ, risking his life to make up for the help you could not give me. Philippians 2:29-30 When there aren't enough finances, there aren't enough workers. Those that do try, get overworked. Because of this, burnout is a growing problem in church leadership in this country. In Israel it destroyed the effectiveness of the leadership. Like Israel, it has affected the leadership and therefore the godliness of our own country.

For it is God's will that by doing good you should silence the ignorant talk of foolish men. 1 Peter 2:15 "Doing good" often has a price tag. When the finances are there, the church can be Christ's hand extended into the world. When the finances aren't there the talk of foolish men goes unanswered. Even foolish men know that the church is supposed to "do good."

As you look at all the issues that people are facing, you can be overwhelmed, even sickened. Many of the world's problems could be solved in months with enough Christian workers and money. The rest would depend on people's response to the Gospel message; a message that millions will never hear before they die. **How, then, can they call on the one they have not believed in? And how can they believe in the one of whom they have not heard? And how can they hear without someone preaching to them? And how can they preach unless they are sent? As it is written, "How beautiful are the feet of those who bring good news!" Romans 10:14-15**

Because you give, the work of the Gospel can go forward. It can go forward on a local level and on a worldwide scale. But it is dependent on people's gifts.

Giving also has ramifications for your personal life. Your level of obedience will also be paving a path for your personal future. You may be paving a smooth path or a stony one.

Remember this: Whoever sows sparingly will also reap sparingly, and whoever sows generously will also reap generously. 2 Corinthians 9:6 Our generosity today will determine the generosity that we receive in the days to come. Remember that you can't give to get. It isn't like playing the slot machines in Las Vegas. Instead, your generous ways will come back to you in a variety of ways, not just finances.

If we put into practice the when, how, and because of giving we will have learned principles for living that will brighten every part of our lives. People will see the same love in us that motivated Jesus to "give" His life as an offering for us. If we don't, we will repeat these lessons over and over again. We must learn these before we are ready for many others.

When You Worship

When they had sung a hymn, they went out to the Mount of Olives.   Mark 14:26 This is one of the few examples of worship in the Gospels.   Yet in its simplicity and location we can learn some of the key aspects of worship.

Jesus and the disciples were headed out to the garden where He will be arrested.   After His arrest, He will be crucified and will die within one day.   Knowing that all this would happen He still worshipped.   Worship isn't based on our circumstance but on the one we are worshipping.   In the New Testament the concept of worship revolves around the fact that God is worthy of worship.

In the wilderness temptation the devil pursued Jesus at His weakest moment.   Satan offered Him incredible power if He would worship him.   **Jesus said to him, "Away from me, Satan!   For it is written: 'Worship the Lord your God, and serve him only.'"   Matthew 4:10** The act of worship secures your allegiance to the object of worship.   When you worship you are setting in motion the most powerful influences your future will have.   **"Worship the Lord your God"**.

When we worship we also fulfill one of the functions that we have as people.   **For we are the temple of the**

living God. 2 Corinthians 6:16b Israel had a stone temple that was destroyed several times in its history. God began the building of a living temple that would never be destroyed when He placed Jesus as the chief cornerstone, **built on the foundation of the apostles and prophets, with Christ Jesus himself as the chief cornerstone. In him the whole building is joined together and rises to become a holy temple in the Lord. And in him you too are being built together to become a dwelling in which God lives by his Spirit. Ephesians 2:20-22**

When we worship we are allowing God to be among us by His Spirit. Since He is no longer dependent on a physical building, God is no longer restricted to one location or country. His love for the world can now be seen and experienced anywhere His people worship.

When we worship we are expressing a truth about our God. He is greater than we are. He did incredible things for us through the sacrifice of His son Jesus. He is involved in our lives on a moment by moment basis. He is God and His creation isn't. When we worship at least a part of the universe is put into its proper perspective.

How You Worship

Jesus declared, "Believe me, woman, a time is coming when you will worship the Father neither on this mountain nor in Jerusalem. You Samaritans worship what you do not know; we worship what we do know, for salvation is from the Jews. Yet a time is coming and has now come when the true worshipers will worship the Father in spirit and truth, for they are the kind of worshipers the Father seeks. God is spirit, and his worshipers must worship in spirit and in truth." John 4:21-24

We must worship **"in spirit and in truth."** That means there is no one form or tradition for worship. If you look at worship, worldwide, you will see an incredible diversity of styles. The criteria for acceptance by God doesn't fall within the variety of worship but rather in the **"spirit and truth"** issue.

Spirit means that part of us that is truly us. Not our outward appearance but our soul, our thoughts, our dreams and desires, us. Truth means that we have not hidden anything from God in the act of worship. We are as exposed to God as we can be. Worship of this kind changes the person worshipping. They are giving honor to God while receiving the impact of His presence.

The style for this will vary from country to country and people to people. Different age groups may prefer different forms. You will see some using few or no instruments while others use everything that exists. None of these are the criteria for true worship. It is an issue of **"spirit and truth."**

There are challenges to this criteria. First, we may be in situations where we have the opportunity to worship but we have concealed things from God. We may be avoiding Him because of circumstances we have not faced and dealt with. In those instances we are called to bring it all out into the open and deal with it before we enter into worship. If we worship outwardly but have not taken care of things inwardly we are not the kind of worshippers He is looking for.

Next, we may find that the spirit part of us isn't focused on God during an opportunity to worship. Instead we are thinking about, worrying about, or contemplating other issues. We might sing, raise our hands, and clap loudly but if we are worrying about other situations then we aren't the kind of worshippers He is looking for.

Both of these challenges take us back to the point of the first white line. We can't love Him if we are letting other things push us away. If we conceal things from Him it shows that we are afraid of Him or unwilling to do something His way. If we spend more mental energy on worrying than worshipping it shows we haven't recognized His role in our lives. He is God and anything we can dream of to worry about is within His capacity to solve.

Instead of the fruitless activities of concealment and worry we need to participate in the bountiful abundance that worship brings. Time in His presence allows Him to encourage and direct us. Wisdom for those tough circumstances can be found while you worship Him. You also are showing Him a level of trust when you worship instead of worry.

He is looking for those who will worship Him in **"spirit and truth."** When He finds them He will be able to pour out on them all that they need to live their lives between the two white lines.

Because You Worship

Jesus answered, "It is written: 'Worship the Lord your God and serve him only.'" Luke 4:8 Service and worship go hand in hand. If you worship God (in spirit and in truth) you will have the strength to serve Him. If you worship God then your priorities will be in proper order and your service to God will be done with the right motivation. Because you worship you can serve Him in the areas He calls you to.

Leaving worship behind will eliminate your capacity to have the strength, motivation, and desire to serve Him in the everyday events of life. So when do we worship God?

We might think that our one chance to worship God is in the Sunday morning church service. That is one chance. We might assume that our personal devotion time could be added to the list of opportunities to worship. That could add seven more times a week. But if we limit our worship time to those settings and situations we are missing one of the key elements of worship.

Worship is the right response to an act or attribute of God that we have seen or experienced. That means we should worship Him many times in any day and multitudes of times on tough days. If we are looking for what He does we will see that He is very active in our lives.

Yes! He is worthy to be worshipped in our devotional time. He is just as worthy of an expression of worship when He reminds us of something before we head out the door for work. When we are spared an accident half way to work we should be praising Him the rest of the way in. If our idea is chosen for the project solution; guess who should get the credit? Worship time again.

Does that mean you need to carry a sound system with you to sing praises? No. Worship is also worth giving. Acknowledging Him and His deeds is an aspect of worship too. **Say to God, "How awesome are your deeds!" Psalm 66:3a**

Be joyful always; pray continually; give thanks in all circumstances, for this is God's will for you in Christ Jesus. 1 Thessalonians 5:16-18

Because you worship this will be possible. Because you worship now you will look forward to Heaven where your greatest acts will be those of worship, **the twenty-four elders fall down before him who sits on the throne, and worship him who lives for ever and ever. They lay their crowns before the throne and say: "You are worthy, our Lord and God, to receive glory and honor and power, for you created all things, and by your will they were created and have their being." Revelation 4:10-11**

When You're Tempted

When tempted, no one should say, "God is tempting me." For God cannot be tempted by evil, nor does he tempt anyone; but each one is tempted when, by his own evil desire, he is dragged away and enticed. Then, after desire has conceived, it gives birth to sin; and sin, when it is full-grown, gives birth to death. James 1:13-15

Treat temptation seriously. Our society may not even call it sin. In fact they may give awards for it. But death awaits those who allow temptation to run its full course.

Scripture lists a variety of behaviors that we are to avoid. This book has several things that we need to learn not to do. Yet we have to see the other side of the temptation coin before we begin to understand how we apply this to our lives.

Going a little farther, he fell with his face to the ground and prayed, "My Father, if it is possible, may this cup be taken from me. Yet not as I will, but as you will." Then he returned to his disciples and found them sleeping. "Could you men not keep watch with me for one hour?" he asked Peter. "Watch and pray so that you will not fall into temptation. The spirit is willing, but the body is weak." Matthew 26:39-41

It can also be very tempting to not do what we are supposed to do. Those issues can be as fatal to our spiritual lives as closing your eyes on the autobahn at a hundred miles an hour.

The struggle doesn't just come down to right and wrong. The struggle comes down to two of the parts that compose every human; the flesh (sinful nature) and the spirit.

So I say, live by the Spirit, and you will not gratify the desires of the sinful nature. For the sinful nature desires what is contrary to the Spirit, and the Spirit what is contrary to the sinful nature. They are in conflict with each other, so that you do not do what you want. But if you are led by the Spirit, you are not under the law. Galatians 5:16-18

When you are tempted you have found an area in your life where the flesh (**sinful nature**) has an influence. To overcome the influence you need to act on several of the rules of the road.

First, God will give you the grace to get past the issue, if you will take the time to go to Him with the issue and seek His help. Trying to hide the issue from Him is a sign of pride. Pride will kill you.

Jesus was seeking God's help the night before He would be crucified. You can seek help from Him any time for any reason. When you go to God for help you are **"living by the Spirit"** and you won't have to do the desires of the sinful nature. When you go make sure you take enough time with Him to get the help you need. Don't just throw up a prayer and hope He catches it. Pray, till you and He have worked it out.

Second, you can have faith that God did not design you for failure. Even though some very important church figures have fallen into temptation you don't have to. Their fall was based on the fact that when they were tempted they didn't go to God for help. It wasn't based on God's inability to help.

Success can be the soil for the weed of pride. This weed like any other chokes out what should have been there, thankfulness. It also covers the ground where the seeds for the future would have been planted.

Everytime we successfully accomplish something for God there is something else waiting for us. He desires to use us to see His kingdom come and His will be done here on earth. We are important to His plans. Each one of these new plans will force us to go to Him in dependence. If it is a God plan then we can't do it by ourselves. We need Him and His people to accomplish it.

Third, you will learn something about yourself from the event. You will find the areas in your life that need to be guarded carefully. For example I have not been tempted in money issues to the same degree I have been tempted in anger issues. That lets me know that I am more likely to be tempted there so I can put up my guard when I see the slightest hint of temptation.

When you are tempted feed the Spirit that He has given us so that it will win the battle and you will win the war against temptation.

How You're Tempted

Do not love the world or anything in the world. If anyone loves the world, the love of the Father is not in him. For everything in the world—the cravings of sinful man, the lust of his eyes and the boasting of what he has and does—comes not from the Father but from the world. 1 John 2:15-16

Temptation can sneak up on you. It isn't always a pile of money sitting in front of you with no one watching. So we are given some warnings about what we crave, watch and say.

People have certain built-in needs. Food is one of them. But too much food can become a heath problem. The wrong kinds of food can complicate the health issue as well. Cravings in this area can lead to those problems.

Cravings exist because they offer a certain amount of satisfaction. Food tastes good. More food can taste good more often. Any area of craving falls into this pattern. But more is not always better or right.

Eyes have a potential to start us down the temptation trail as well. We see something and it becomes fuel for our imaginations. We want it before it is ours to have. We want it even if it isn't ours to have. When we want it like that, it is easy to lose our focus on Jesus. Looking at the wrong things as you drive down the autobahn can lead to some scary experiences for you and those on the road with you.

We have probably all watched someone ahead of us on the road weave and drift in and out of their lane because they weren't focused on the it. The lust of the eyes can be in any area of life but it always produces the same result—danger to the driver and those on the road with them.

When you see something you need to evaluate it in light of the scriptures so you know what to do with it. Do I ignore it? Do I work towards it? Is it something He will arrange or do I have to make it happen? Seeing is believing. What you believe about what you see should reflect what God has said about it.

Boasting and pride are brothers. When these two get together you are guaranteed some trouble. On the autobahn they can be fatal. A family trait of these two is that they don't need anyone's help, observations or input—including God's.

Let these traits be a warning sign to you or for others. You may need a good eye to eye chat with the creator of the universe (your heavenly Father) or an honest look at how your successful deeds were really accomplished. Any way it happens it needs to. For others you may find that taking them to that point can be difficult. Difficult or not if you have a relationship with them, do it. This temptation can lead to every other one in time.

Because You're Tempted

So, if you think you are standing firm, be careful that you don't fall! No temptation has seized you except what is common to man. And God is faithful; he will not let you be tempted beyond what you can bear. But when you are tempted, he will also provide a way out so that you can stand up under it. 1 Corinthians 10:12-13

Every point of temptation becomes an opportunity to grow. With each temptation He will **"provide a way out."** Learning those **"ways"** will enable you to avoid the possible sin but also enable you to help others. Jesus modeled that for us with His life.

For this reason he had to be made like his brothers in every way, in order that he might become a merciful and faithful high priest in service to God, and that he might make atonement for the sins of the people. Because he himself suffered when he was tempted, he is able to help those who are being tempted. Hebrews 2:17-18

His temptation examples show us how to deal with temptation and grow as we drive the **"way out."** When Jesus was tempted in the desert by Satan (Matthew 4:1-11), He quoted and applied scripture that applied to that situation. Having and applying truth is always a part of the **"way out."**

If I need something but can't afford it I might be tempted to steal it if the opportunity arose. That temptation can be combated by applying the truth, **"But seek first his kingdom and his righteousness, and all these thing will be given to you as well." Matthew 6:33** Let God provide. You spend your energy expanding His kingdom.

If sexual temptations come you can apply Matthew 5:28 and 1 John 1:9. **But I tell you that anyone who looks at a woman lustfully has already committed adultery with her in his heart. Matthew 5:28 If we confess our sins, he is faithful and just and will forgive us our sins and purify us from all unrighteousness. 1 John 1:9** Applying those truths will humble you, bringing you closer to the first white line. His impact in your life will minimize temptation's draw.

That application will be at least a part of the **"way out."** We may also need to look at why we are tempted. **In the spring, at the time when kings go off to war, David sent Joab out with the king's men and the whole Israelite army. 2 Samuel 11:1a** David wasn't where he belonged. Bathsheba would come into sight soon and the lust of the eyes and the cravings of the flesh would lead to the death of many things in David's life. David was the king and **"In the spring of the year when kings go off to war,"** David didn't go.

One of the best defenses against temptation is to be fully involved in what God has asked you to do. Working with Him and facing the struggles that obedience brings helps you to stay focused on what is important. That focus will enable you to drive past temptation along the road you and God are building.

Several years ago I was praying with someone who had struggled in a certain area of temptation for years. As I asked questions to understand the situation it was revealed that they weren't doing what God wanted them to do with their life. There were no solutions until that changed. When we aren't on the autobahn we will face temptations that only the jungle around us can generate. We are in an area of influence that will ultimately be fatal.

Submit yourselves, then, to God. Resist the devil, and he will flee from you. Come near to God and he will come near to you. Wash your hands, you sinners, and purify your hearts, you double-minded. Grieve, mourn and wail. Change your laughter to mourning and your joy to gloom. Humble yourselves before the Lord, and he will lift you up. James 4:7-10

Temptation can also be a byproduct of doing the right things. A couple may separate for a time while doing two projects for God. But if they don't take the time to reunite regularly the sexual temptations can seem overwhelming. Some mission organizations will not allow their people to be separated from a spouse past certain time limits to deal with that potential problem. So dealing with the why is also important.

Pornography is another "why" that has to be dealt with too. The **"lustful look"** passage in Matthew 5:28 also needs to be applied to images not just people. We will have to constantly deal with what we see. TV programming, literature and computer images all have the potential of putting us into tempting situations. Avoiding these will be a part of the **"way out"** as well.

Take the time to look Jesus in the eye as He leads you through the variety of **"way outs"** and thank Him. Because of His life and death He understands temptation and you.

Stay on the Path

Then Jesus went through the towns and villages, teaching as he made his way to Jerusalem. Someone asked him, "Lord, are only a few people going to be saved?" He said to them, "Make every effort to enter through the narrow door, because many, I tell you, will try to enter and will not be able to." Luke 13:22-24

Jesus answered, "I am the way and the truth and the life. No one comes to the Father except through me." John 14:6 Jesus is that narrow door; He is only one-person wide.

At this point you are probably starting to see just how narrow of a door Jesus is. His ways are not like anyone else's. As you put His ways into practice and begin to build the pavement and add the paint, you start to stand out. Like Jesus said, **"You are the light of the world. A city on a hill cannot be hidden." Matthew 5:14**

If people are lost in the dark and looking for a way out, you have become a source of hope and relief. Those who are hiding in the dark, who have chosen the deeds of darkness as a lifestyle, don't respond the same way. You force them to see themselves for what they really are.

"Then you will be handed over to be persecuted and put to death, and you will be hated by all nations

because of me. At that time many will turn away from the faith and will betray and hate each other, and many false prophets will appear and deceive many people. Because of the increase of wickedness, the love of most will grow cold, but he who stands firm to the end will be saved. And this gospel of the kingdom will be preached in the whole world as a testimony to all nations, and then the end will come. Matthew 24:9-14

There are more people killed for their Christian faith (about a quarter of a million people a year) today than at any other time in history. Each one of them found the narrow door and the path that leads to the Father behind it. They all started down that path. Each one began building the ways of Christ into their lives. At some point that "light" became unbearable for someone and they shut it off. They probably tried to convince the Christian to voluntarily turn out the light first-to deny their allegiance to the narrow door. When they didn't, the "light" was destroyed.

Though the destruction to the individual is complete, the spirit of the martyr suffered no damage, **"but he who stands firm to the end will be saved."**

On the road we build, there will be a variety of obstacles. They will vary from country-to-country. In Muslim nations, Christians often face death. In prosperous nations, Christians face materialism, pride, immorality, envy, or compromise.

If any of these get us off the roadway, we don't find the gas stations we need for the grace that will get us past these obstacles. If we stay on the pavement, we have all the supplies we need to do the good works we were created for-and if needed, die a good death.

"And this gospel of the kingdom will be preached in the whole world as a testimony to all nations, and then the end will come." Matthew 24:14

As you travel on God's highway you will encounter people who need Jesus. They need what you have learned as you paved and painted your highway. Your knowledge represents hope for them.

Some of us will be asked to build our road to faraway places. Other will build theirs close to home. Some will be missionaries and evangelists. Others will stay and spread the gospel at home, while supporting those that go in prayer and finances.

How you contribute to the spread of the gospel will be dependent on the road that God has planned for you. Only your daily steps on the highway will allow you to clearly understand your part.

Do not conform any longer to the pattern of this world, but be transformed by the renewing of your mind. Then you will be able to test and approve what God's will is—his good, pleasing and perfect will. Romans 12:2

Open for Business

How many times have you tried to determine if a business was open or not? You're in a strange town, it's an odd day, or your schedule is a bit early; are they open for business? You look for lights, the sign that there is life and therefore open for business.

"Then the righteous will shine like the sun in the kingdom of their Father. He who has ears, let him hear. Matthew 13:43

When we are living in right relationship with our Heavenly Father, it shows. It doesn't just show by what happens to us but by how what happens to us affects us. Do we shine? A light plugged into the power shines when the switch is on.

After six days Jesus took with him Peter, James and John the brother of James, and led them up a high mountain by themselves. There he was transfigured before them. His face shone like the sun, and his clothes became as white as the light. Matthew 17:1-2

Jesus went off to pray on a regular basis. This time he took some disciples. They saw the light in a new way, reflected from the Father.

"Let your light shine before men, that they may see your good deeds, and praise your Father in heaven." Matthew 5:16

If you have spent time with the Father before you do things, you will shine that reflected light just like Jesus did. Our time in the presence of Father God will change us "and glorify your Father who is in heaven."

When Moses came down from Mount Sinai with the two tablets of the Testimony in his hands, he was not aware that his face was radiant because he had spoken with the Lord. Exodus 34:29

Moses "was not aware that his face was radiant because he had spoken with the Lord." You may not be aware either. Others will be. You can't replace that radiance with anything else. Only time spent in God's presence will give the glow. Then people will know, you're open for business, the kingdom's business.

You can spend your life doing a million things. If you start each day in our Father God's presence, if you hug that white line, you will always do one of God's million things. If you begin days without time in His presence then your activity may be wasted. You may be busy but you won't be open for business, not God's business anyway.

"When these things begin to take place, stand up and lift up your heads, because your redemption is drawing near." Luke 21:28

If you find yourself active but not open, "stand up and lift up your heads." Look our Heavenly Father straight in the eye, ask forgiveness, and fall into His arms. You can't reflect and shine what you haven't been around.

Soon we will be painting the second white line: loving people. But don't forget this first white line. Without it to guide us the second white line becomes impossible to paint.

Everything and Anything

"If you can?" said Jesus. "*Everything* is possible for him who believes." Immediately the boy's father exclaimed, "I do believe; help me overcome my unbelief!" Mark 9:23-24 (Italics mine)

Miracles and many of the other bigger-than-life occurrences in the New Testament can be a mystery to us. How? Why? Why not? When? Now? Me? All are questions that arise.

I tell you the truth, anyone who has faith in me will do what I have been doing. He will do even greater things than these, because I am going to the Father. And I will do whatever you ask in my name, so that the Son may bring glory to the Father. You may ask me for *anything* in my name, and I will do it. John 14:12-14 (Italics mine)

So how does all this work today? The same way it did then. If you look at Hebrews chapter eleven you will find a long list of people who accomplished the *"everything"* and *"anything"* events of the Old Testament. Abel, Enoch, Noah, Abraham, Isaac, Jacob, Joseph, Moses, Rahab, Gideon, Barak, Samson, Jephthah, David, Samuel, and the prophets are all listed there.

The **"faith"** that they had came from their relationship with God. Time spent in an awesome God's presence produced the heart, mind, and direction for the extraordinary. There is a church in South Korea that has nearly three-quarters of a million people in it. That church is impacting the country and world. There is none like it. So how did the founder get the idea? He is known for spending time with God (about four hours a day) in prayer.

Time spent in God's presence purifies the motives of your heart. You won't be able to ask for something that isn't His desire after enough time in His presence. With enough time in His presence, you will begin to see the situation His way and respond accordingly. Faith blossoms in that kind of soil, watered with God's presence. What you become and do with your life will be determined to a great extent by those who influence you most.

Everyone could have Father God as his or her greatest influence. If they did, they would attempt the *"everythings"* and *"anythings."* Failures would only send them back to the Father for some more understanding. And as Jesus said, **"He will do even greater things than these, because I am going to the Father."** John 14:12b

The *"everythings"* and *"anythings"* won't happen overnight but the list will begin to grow. In time, you will be able to relate to people in the Bible; not only for their failure, but also in the *"everythings"* and *"anythings"* that Father God would like to wrap your life in. Jesus proved to the boy's father that there was help for his unbelief; nothing has changed.

Jesus Christ is the same yesterday and today and forever. Hebrews 13:8 Continue to pave and paint in the open space that repentance bought. What God has for you is more than you can imagine.

Being Perfect

Be perfect, therefore, as your heavenly Father is perfect. Matthew 5:48 Ready to wrestle? We know you can throw a "perfect" game in baseball. We know that you can find the "perfect" outfit for an event. You can even get "perfect" weather. But being "perfect" like God? There are people that destroy their lives in their pursuit of perfection. So how do we deal with this one?

First let's look at the word perfect. When it's used in the Bible like this, it means *completion.* That *every potential it possesses has been realized.* Simply stated, it means that you *wholeheartedly* obey. That's the word perfect.

Now the context of the word. Jesus has just spent ten verses (Matthew 5:38-47) telling us how to deal with our **"enemies."** He concludes that we must **"love your enemies," "pray for those who persecute you,"** and openly **"greet"** them. After all that, Jesus commands us to be **"perfect, therefore, as your heavenly Father is perfect."**

When these two thoughts meet, it should produce this kind of an understanding; God loves those who hate Him. We need to whole-heartedly do the same.

Examples of this are scattered throughout the Bible. In the Old Testament we can read about Elisha (2 Kings 6:8-23). An army is hunting Elisha. They have orders to capture him. At night they surround the city where he is staying. When he is made aware of the problem, Elisha prays and the entire enemy force goes blind.

At this point he could have easily had them destroyed. Instead he **"prepared a great feast for them, and after they had finished eating and drinking, he sent them away, and they returned to their master."** 2 **Kings 6:23a**

After a brutal beating, corrupt court session, and the public humiliation and intense physical pain of the cross (Luke 22:63-23:34) Jesus calls out, **"Father, forgive them, for they do not know what they are doing."** **Luke 23:34a**

Soon after Jesus was buried and resurrected, one of His converts, Stephen, begins to preach all over Jerusalem. He is so successful that he is hated by the local Jews. In fact, they have a mock trial for him and stone him to death. His last words are, **"Lord, do not hold this sin against them."** Acts 7:60

Loving our enemies is how we obey the command to be **"perfect."** This final command we learn from the first white line also gets us started on the commands for the second white line, **"loving your neighbor as yourself."** Everything that we have looked at up to this point means nothing if you don't learn how to love people as much as you love God.

If anyone says, "I love God," yet hates his brother, he is a liar. For anyone who does not love his brother, whom he has seen, cannot love God, whom he has not seen. And he has given us this command: Whoever loves God must also love his brother." 1 **John 4:20-21**

We know this isn't normal or natural. But like the first white line, this one can be obeyed as we learn to live the super-natural life that Jesus makes possible for us on the highway He is trying to build in our lives. As both white lines are painted, we will be guided to all that God has intended for our lives. We become lives where **"all mankind will see God's salvation."**

Painting the Second White Line

"Love your neighbor as yourself."

Matthew 22:39

Love Your ...

Up to this point we have looked at how we can love the Lord our God with all our heart, mind, soul, and strength. Now we turn our attention to the people that are ours to love. Those people will have many titles. Some are titles of familiarity: neighbor, husband, wife, children, mother, dad, or brother. Others are titles we try to avoid: enemy, tax collector, politician, master, or persecutor. No matter the title, the commands of the second white line will guide us towards loving the people behind the titles.

If we have learned to follow the guidance of the first white line, the second white line is attainable. If we ever leave our first set of commands, we will be crushed under the second. Jesus put them in their priority for a purpose. You can't love all the people you will face in life if you don't face the God who came to bring us life first.

We love because he first loved us. 1 John 4:19 Your daily experiences with the first white line will allow you to see and fulfill the realities of the second one. **And so we know and rely on the love God has for us. 1 John 4:16a** In many respects God hands us a baton of love that we pass on to the next person we encounter. We rely on what we receive from Him in order to have something to pass on.

Love is a perishable commodity. So we must replenish daily. Staying close to the first white line will keep the supply lines open, no matter what we are facing. **We do not want you to be uninformed, brothers, about the hardships we suffered in the province of Asia. We were under great pressure, far beyond our ability to endure so that we despaired even of life. Indeed, in our hearts we felt the sentence of death. But this happened that we might not rely on ourselves but on God, who raises the dead. He has delivered us from such a deadly peril, and he will deliver us. On him we have set our hope that he will continue to deliver us, as you help us by your prayers. Then many will give thanks on our behalf for the gracious favor granted us in answer to the prayers of many. 2 Corinthians 1:8-11**

As you embark on the second set of commands don't forget, neglect, or ignore what you have made a part of your life already. **Love the Lord your God with all your heart and with all your soul and with all your mind and with all your strength. Mark 12:30**

The Dangers of Love

A sewing needle belongs with some thread and fabric. It has no business exploring an electrical socket. The first use is constructive while the second application can be fatal. Love holds the same capacity. It is intended to be an all-consuming experience with God and people. You can take God's love and squander it on yourself, your possessions, or positions.

For the love of money is a root of all kinds of evil. Some people, eager for money, have wandered from the faith and pierced themselves with many griefs.
1 Timothy 6:10

People love money because they see the power and possibilities behind it. They don't see the pitfalls. With wealth comes responsibility, time loss, the crime magnet, a potential loss of dependency on God, and the unsettling knowledge that it could all be gone in a day.

It also seems to create an appetite for more. There is always just a little bit more out there that you could have with just a little bit more money. What you end up trading for that money could cost you everything.

Do not love the world or anything in the world. If anyone loves the world, the love of the Father is not in

him. 1 John 2:15 What good is it for a man to gain the whole world, yet forfeit his soul? Mark 8:36

When we have received God's love, it is intended to be used for ourselves and others: people. Remember the two white lines, love God and love people. If we start to fix our focus on positions or possessions, we are looking past people. When that happens people get run over and Christ's name is muddied. God's purposes for your life and others are wasted. People begin to look past you and see only your money. In time you may end up trading in your eternal reward for the earthly pleasures. Jesus said, **"It is easier for a camel to go through the eye of a needle than for a rich man to enter the kingdom of God." Mark 10:25**

Love God and love people. If you happen to acquire wealth then you will have a natural outlet for it in the needs you see in God's kingdom and the people around you. If you don't continue to love God and people, you will start to put on the weight that wealth brings. That begins to destroy your spiritual health just like the extra pounds do your physical heath. Stay in shape physically; work out. Stay in shape spiritually; give out.

Love Not Lust

"But I tell you that anyone who looks at a woman lustfully has already committed adultery with her in his heart. Matthew 5:28

Every year the damage of adultery is experienced by millions of families worldwide. Divorce, STD's, broken trust, shattered children, and rage crimes are all a part of the damage report. Sadly all of this destruction was initiated by a simple little look, a second look.

Within the context of marriage the sexual act is a bonding and blending event. Two lives come together and share in the most intimate setting.

Outside of marriage it is a dangerous carnival ride, full of thrills and chills. Much like the adrenaline junkies who look for a new experience, a new high, adultery becomes not just an event, but a way of life. Why deal with a long-term relationship and all the hassles when you can have the thrills for free?

Love is well described in the scriptures. Lust is also explained. **It is God's will that you should be sanctified; that you should avoid sexual immorality; that each of you should learn to control his own body in a way that is holy and honorable, not in passionate lust like the heathen, who do not know God; and that in this matter**

no one should wrong his brother or take advantage of him. The Lord will punish men for all such sins, as we have already told you and warned you. For God did not call us to be impure, but to live a holy life. 1 Thessalonians 4:3-7

Lust means too much, too soon, too fast, or too often. You marry one person, therefore, two is too much. Before marriage is too soon, over fifty percent of all engagements break up, and statistics show that those who live together before marriage have a higher divorce rate that those who don't.

Within the boundaries of marriage a couple will still have to learn to live in love not lust as the damage from too fast or too often can add up and lead to serious marital problems. Love is patient, lust demands, it is too fast.

Too often people don't realize the bonding and blending capacity of sex. For one of the two it may only be an event, like a roller-coaster ride, but for the other there is a bonding and blending. Abused too often this bonding and blending capacity is scarred. In time the capacity is lost all together.

Scripturally we see what happened when David let the simple little look (2 Samuel 11) turn into an adulterous event with Bathsheba. **"This is what the Lord says: 'Out of your own household I am going to bring calamity upon you. Before your very eyes I will take your wives and give them to one who is close to you, and he will lie with your wives in broad daylight. You did it in secret, but I will do this thing in broad daylight before all Israel. 2 Samuel 12:11-12**

David's sin of adultery pushed the first domino in a long line of many. As they fell one disastrous event after another followed within his personal family and his kingdom. Before he would die there would be incest in the home, one of his sons would rebel and try to take the throne, Israel would divide itself from Judah, and the list goes on and on and on.

Lust always leads to destruction. Learn to live in control of yourself. If you struggle with the second look get good at the confession of adultery. Going to the throne of God for forgiveness will begin that process of changing your heart from a lustful one to a loving one. It will also allow you to get the grace and mercy (Hebrews 4:16) you need to love the people in your world.

Love Your Neighbor as Yourself

"The second is this: 'Love your neighbor as yourself.' There is no commandment greater than these." **Mark 12:31** Generally speaking, the Jewish culture had a capacity to love themselves. They knew they were God's chosen children, created in His image. Each child was seen as a gift from God. These truths were reinforced as the adults invested in the children. The young men learned a skill as an apprentice beginning at age twelve and the young ladies, skills for the home. At an early age they were contributing parts of society. That platform of emotional security created a foundation that love could build on. They could love themselves and once touched by God they could love others. That changes cultures.

Today we find we have to take a step backwards so that we can see why this very first command may be so difficult for some. Instead of a special place in society and the knowledge that they are created and chosen by God, many people grow up with just the opposite understanding. Too many children grow-up thinking that they were "a mistake" from birth. Born out of time with their siblings, out of wedlock, or from an illegitimate relationship, children constantly know that they aren't wanted; after all, they were not planned. This is reinforced by an intense rejection if a divorce follows.

For those who are spared this experience, other traps are waiting ahead. The culture in the United States of America is laced with competition. You must try out for sports, parts in plays, jobs, educational paths, and relationships. You will find the opportunity to be rejected in almost any area of your life. In time those rejections take a toll on you and you find it hard to love what has been rejected so many times before.

Not everyone is subject to this. Those who do succeed, those who are chosen, can do well. Others who are raised in areas where the population is smaller and the competition is little or none can escape the cultural traps. If they can build a foundation of security before the competition gets too tough, they can love themselves, too.

Sin is one of the other traps that people aren't warned about anymore. When you sin the Holy Spirit immediately begins to convict you (John 16:8) and attempts to lead you to the cross of Christ where you can be forgiven (Colossians 2:13-15). Not knowing about sin doesn't stop the work of the Holy Spirit. This spiritual pressure on an individual who doesn't believe, understand, or know of the spiritual realm is confusing. This can lead to a lot of self-destructive behavior.

Since sin is not an agreed-upon truth anymore, many people are trying to live life with its consequences all around them, but no honest solutions. This taints any human heart and makes it difficult for them to honestly love themselves.

Unexplained evil also has a powerful influence on those who have been exposed to it. Sexual abuse, violent crime, the horrors of war, and cultic rituals can leave a person with a sense of hopelessness. They feel marked.

Somehow these people think they deserved it, caused it, or had it coming. If there was a God where was He then?

Each of these traps forces us to take a step backwards before we can move forward between the two white lines. Gaining a scriptural understanding of those events will allow us to see that God had warned the world about these kinds of events. These events are possible when individuals or whole nations turn their backs on Him and His ways. Innocent victims are always the result of someone's sin.

If you are struggling with this first command of loving your neighbor, stop. Look back at the first line and let God's love for you grow. Then venture out and love your neighbor as God has loved you. In time you will see yourself the way God does. Then this first command will take on a whole new meaning. It will become a source of joy as you reach out to those who feel the way you used to.

Love your neighbor as yourself. Jesus gave us another commandment that helps to clarify this one; **"So in everything, do to others what you would have them do to you, for this sums up the Law and the Prophets." Matthew 7:12** Now, you can step down the road and know the freedom that those two white lines define.

If You Love One Another

"A new commandment I give you: Love one another. As I have loved you, so you must love one another. All men will know that you are my disciples if you love one another." John 13:34-35 Jesus was speaking to his disciples. They knew everything about each other because they lived together for three plus years. That doesn't make it easy to **"love one another."** Yet Christ knew that **"if you love one another,"** **"all men will know that you are my disciples."** Things haven't changed. If a church is full of people who do love one another then it becomes a magnet that draws people to Jesus. If it isn't, if it's full of people acting like everyone else, it repels people. They become disgusted with organized religion and usually miss Jesus.

A place like this reinforces the love that God has for us. Being loved by God and His people will fill a person's love bowl. It becomes easy for them to give from that abundance.

Why aren't all churches like this? Jesus practices open adoption. He adopts the immature, dishonest, rude, and vulgar people of this earth. People like you and me. Then he puts them all together and points them in the same direction and calls it a church. See why we have problems in the church sometimes? We have to love God, to be able to love others.

Once people are in the church you have to deal with what the enemy did to them while they were in his camp. You have to work with gifts that aren't like yours. All these issues force you back to the first white line; back to the love of God. It is a simple concept on paper but sometimes difficult to obey in the daily areas of life. When you are hurt, lied about, forgotten, annoyed, or washed in someone's wake, it can be tough. Jesus understands, he had all of this happen to him on a daily basis. He coped in the same way we must; He prayed and got in touch with His Heavenly Father.

Your highway will include long stretches that are signed "church." You will worship there, raise your kids, give there, and donate thousands of hours as a volunteer. Learning to love that collection of people is a life-long endeavor. You will need to use a lot of paint to cover those long stretches of pavement.

Love Lost-Divorce

Some Pharisees came to him to test him. They asked, "Is it lawful for a man to divorce his wife for any and every reason?"

"Haven't you read," he replied, "that at the beginning the Creator 'made them male and female,' and said, 'For this reason a man will leave his father and mother and be united to his wife, and the two will become one flesh'? So they are no longer two, but one. Therefore what God has joined together, let man not separate."

"Why then," they asked, "did Moses command that a man give his wife a certificate of divorce and send her away?"

Jesus replied, "Moses permitted you to divorce your wives because your hearts were hard. But it was not this way from the beginning. I tell you that anyone who divorces his wife, except for marital unfaithfulness, and marries another woman commits adultery." Matthew 19:3-9

"Hard hearts" and "adultery" produce divorce. Hugging the first white line will prevent us from these two fatal traps. Hearts become hard when the pain of life isn't healed on a regular basis. Our burdens, cares, worries, and pain need to be taken to our Heavenly Father as they happen. If we let Him apply first aid then we can know that it will only be a temporary wound-not a life long issue.

If we let the wound fester we run the risk of a hard heart. People who pledged to love each other "until death do they part" will change their minds if little issues are left alone. When several others join one little issue the total amount can be overwhelming-too much for the heart to bear. Hardness sets in at that point.

Adultery is also often the by-product of a hard heart. One partner is hurt by the other and doesn't go to the Great Physician (God). So when someone else is nice to them they are attracted to them. That sets the stage for the act of adultery.

It also happens if we haven't spent the time with God that creates the opposite of a hard heart-a sensitive heart. Sensitive hearts see sin coming and respond appropriately. Adultery is sin no matter how a culture views it. But a hard heart will see it the way it wants to.

I have lived in the same town since 1970. In that time I have watched the rising death toll on love lost-resulting in divorce. You could tell your own stories just like I can. You've seen the children who seemed to go from good to bad overnight because of a divorce. Men and women, leaders in the church, have hardened their hearts through neglect. The resulting acts of adultery show that they had left their first love behind (Jesus) and tried to find fulfillment in His work.

Without the love of God you will sooner or later run out of love for the people in your world. If it is a spouse then you run the risk of the adultery and/or the divorce issue.

What if you have already experienced the tragedy of divorce? Like any mess it can be difficult to clean up. You will have to accept whatever responsibility you had in it to begin with. There are so many different possibilities of the why and how that they can't all be covered in a book like this. But cleansing your conscience before God is the start. Once you have done that then you need to apply the Commands of Christ that you haven't. Steady work will clear what rubble is yours.

From that point you can go forward and know that God has been working with messes since He created us. He redeemed us from our sin and He can redeem you from this one.

Love Your Enemies

Most of us have not been involved in a military conflict, where you have an enemy who is trying to destroy you and you, them. So our concept of an enemy is usually limited. But we do have an enemy who is trying to destroy us as individuals and the church as a functioning body. Satan does all he can and uses anyone he can to accomplish his goals for our lives. In the church, his power is based on the pressure he can bring upon it from people. In some countries the church is experiencing extreme persecution because of Satan's influence in lives. Martyrs die daily around the world because of it.

In countries where religious exercise is protected, Satan uses another tactic. He influences immature individuals within the church to divide those who are trying to obey Christ. In many settings your worst opposition will come from those within the church. That internal friction can lead to church splits, ineffective ministries, and a bad name for the cause of Christ.

So learning to love your enemy may include a variety of scenarios. They may come to your church door with machine guns or they may sit next to you in the pew and shake your hand every Sunday morning. Jesus' command for both these situations is the same. It takes the guesswork out of it and removes us from the seat of critic into the seat that Christ occupied: the compassionate.

"But I tell you who hear me: Love your enemies, do good to those who hate you, bless those who curse you, pray for those who mistreat you. If someone strikes you on one cheek, turn to him the other also. If someone takes your cloak, do not stop him from taking your tunic. Give to everyone who asks you, and if anyone takes what belongs to you, do not demand it back. Do to others as you would have them do to you.

If you love those who love you, what credit is that to you? Even 'sinners' love those who love them. And if you do good to those who are good to you, what credit is that to you? Even 'sinners' do that. And if you lend to those from whom you expect repayment, what credit is that to you? Even 'sinners' lend to 'sinners' expecting to be repaid in full. But love your enemies, do good to them, and lend to them without expecting to get anything back. Then your reward will be great, and you will be sons of the Most High, because he is kind to the ungrateful and wicked. Be merciful, just as your Father is merciful." Luke 6:27-36

Where there is an aggressive or passive action from an enemy, Jesus has established an active counterattack of love. In these verses He commanded us to **"do good, bless, pray for, do not stop him from taking your tunic, give, lend, and be merciful."** Those are impossible human emotions in the settings that have been described. Impossible, unless we are hugging that first white line and passing on to our enemies what we have received from our Heavenly Father.

As soon as we see someone as "an enemy," that is our warning to re-focus our eyes on Jesus (Hebrews 12:1-3) and see the situation His way. Then we need to ask Him for His strategy to love these people. If you do it, then Jesus can get "your enemy's" attention and work in their lives. At the cross Jesus said, **"Father, forgive them, for they do not know what they are doing."** Luke 23:34a Moments after His death one of those Jesus had just prayed for responded this way. **The centurion, seeing what had happened, praised God and said, "Surely this was a righteous man." Luke 23:47.**

If we respond any other way, our attacker seems justified in his actions. It just fixes their focus of hatred on us. This usually leads to an escalation of the conflict, which can split churches, marriages, and bring intense persecution where there might not have been any. This can minimize conflict. But Christ's commands don't guarantee an absence of persecution; they just guarantee that you will represent Christ in it. **"I have told you these things, so that in me you may have peace. In this world you will have trouble. But take heart! I have overcome the world." John 16:33**

As you represent Christ to your enemies, there won't be any place in you to adopt their attitudes, actions, or attributes.

When You're Angry

"You have heard that it was said to the people long ago, 'Do not murder, and anyone who murders will be subject to judgement.' But I tell you that anyone who is angry with his brother will be subject to judgment. Again, anyone who says to his brother, "Raca," is answerable to the Sanhedrin. But anyone who says, 'You fool!' will be in danger of the fire of hell. Matthew 5:21-23

As you can see, Jesus takes a serious view on how we deal with our anger. If people paid any attention to this we might not have the constant factor of destruction that unchecked anger generates.

In contrast, showing no anger in a deserving situation can be immature as well. Getting angry is not the problem. Jesus was angry numerous times in the Gospels. What happens next can be the problem. Jesus says that taking anger to the wrong course of action ("Raca, or, you fool") is dangerous. In fact He says it can start something that can lead to Hell.

"In your anger do not sin": Do not let the sun go down while you are still angry, and do not give the devil a foothold. Ephesians 4:26-27

When you are angry you are at a crossroads in life. What you do with it will have a direct impact on your present situation and future. You need to start an evaluation process by asking yourself "why?" There are four basic instigators for anger. First is the favored, "I'm right, they're wrong" situation. Next is the least favorite, "They're right and I'm wrong" reality. Then there are the confusing, "We're both right" and it's counterpart "We're both wrong."

Next you need to see if the issue or setting warrants the response. Babies are not born with coordination capabilities, thus their constant capacity to break everything they touch. If we are getting angry over that then we have forgotten some of the realities of life. Our anger in those types of setting is immature.

Many issues are not legitimate fuels for anger and action. Instead they come from our embarrassment over being wrong. Or we have decided some insignificant issue needs to become a battlefield. Either of these shows our immaturity.

A man's wisdom gives him patience; it is to his glory to overlook an offense. Proverbs 19:11 Just the evaluation process will cause many of us to change our current way of dealing with anger causing events.

How You're Angry

As you have seen anger is a normal healthy response to certain events in life. It is also a maturity issue. Here are the stages of anger that each one of us will need to work through as we learn how to deal with the anger within in a fashion that honors Jesus.

The temper tantrum is the first level. It is basic, raw emotion, directed at no one person. The floor that often receives the fury has nothing to do with the emotion. In adults it might look more like this. **So Ahab (the king) went home, sullen and angry because Naboth the Jezreelite had said, "I will not give you the inheritance of my fathers." He lay on his bed sulking and refused to eat. 1 Kings 21:4**

A little farther up the maturity scale is the hit and grunt stage. Here the anger produces a physical reaction towards someone else. Although this is more mature (people understand that someone is involved) it is not an acceptable method in any circumstance.

Next is an event called the point and shout. The angry person or parties engage in a shouting match that is often accompanied by the pointing of fingers. It is less harmful than the hit and grunt but solves nothing.

Each of these first three stages shows us some basic factors about how we deal with anger. We are not creative when we are angry. We undergo a neurological block that prevents our creative energies from entering the problem. That is good. It is like a safety valve. If we were creative and angry at the same time we would have more scary episodes in life than we currently do. Instead of creativity we either do nothing (often demonstrated by a prancing back and forth without any intelligent talk) or pour out our bucket of left over ideas from past experiences where we thought about what we could have, should have done, after the fact.

If we do nothing the issue deescalates. If we pour out the bucket things often get worse fast. Nothing also helps describe the fourth level called silence. This stage is a necessary one to accomplish along the way to the final stage that represents mature anger. Silence works to a certain degree but it cannot be considered a long-term solution.

People around you will in time be frustrated. Others will learn to take advantage of your silence. All of these will accelerate the possibilities of your silence turning into an emotional, physical, or health problem.

Young men tend to get stuck in this phase. Growing up they are outmatched by most women their age in verbal skills. This along with their uniquely awkward stage of voice development (the squeaky, "is that your mother speaking phase") results in silence as a stage that is occupied until it becomes a problem.

Men have a tendency to stay silent until they feel that action is necessary. The only level they have accomplished up to this point is level three; the point and shout. Unfortunately, the point and shout becomes the point and shoot. Men are cataclysmic when they get angry and don't know how to deal with it.

Women tend to get past this stage and falter on the fifth stage; try to say it right and it comes out wrong. Because you aren't creative and angry at the same time any words at this point will only be destructive to the overall situation. In their desire to preserve relationships and solve problems they create a deeper wedge and drive away those involved. Failure at this level typically drives them back to the silent stage.

As awkward and destructive as this phase can be it must be mastered. Never trying will result in the prison of silence. So prepare yourself and those around you for this stage. If you can warn them ahead of time it will accomplish at least two things. First you will have already talked to them about the anger issue. The next time will probably be easier. Then for them they will understand that you are trying to grow up and deal with the issue. An attempt is always better understood if people know what the issue is.

Mature anger is characterized by three words and modeled by God Himself. Time, place, and solution are the key words and God modeled them this way. Two thousand years ago, in Jerusalem, He allowed His son to be crucified. In that time and at that place He let His righteous anger toward our sin be fully fulfilled with the death of His son.

When angry we have the privilege of getting our solutions from God if we will take the time to do it. **If any of you lacks wisdom, he should ask God, who gives generously to all without finding fault, and it will be given to him. James 1:5**

Armed with God's answer (remember it could be that you were wrong) we can pick a time and place to deal with the issue. Having the right answer must also be accompanied by having the right attitude. **Instead, speaking the truth in love, we will in all things grow up**

into him who is the Head, that is, Christ. Ephesians 4:15

Anger can be a catalyst for positive change or it can be the destructive force we see in the headlines everyday.

Because You're Angry

Anger often signals the need for some kind of change. **Jesus said to the man with the shriveled hand, "Stand up in front of everyone."**

Then Jesus asked them, "Which is lawful on the Sabbath: to do good or to do evil, to save life or to kill?" But they remained silent.

He looked around at them in anger and, deeply distressed at their stubborn hearts, said to the man, "Stretch out your hand." He stretched it out, and his hand was completely restored. Then the Pharisees went out and began to plot with the Herodians how they might kill Jesus. Mark 3:3-6

Church had become a ritual. It was not a place to learn about God or His ways. Instead the leaders had composed a complex set of rules without any of the characteristics of the God they were trying to honor. These rules made it impossible to **"do good."** Something had to change.

Jesus changed things without any of the damage that an immature display of anger would bring. The Pharisees and Herodians meanwhile decided that murder was the only way to deal with it. They didn't want the change. Their anger would result in Christ's death. Anger becomes a catalyst for change. If you are mature, it is a change in the right direction. Immaturity produces change but in the wrong ways. Either the situation gets worse or a confrontation is delayed and probably escalated. Waiting is appropriate if you are waiting for God's time, place, and solution. Delaying without God's intervention only sets the stage for more trouble.

The biggest challenge comes to us when we could avoid the whole situation altogether. It is someone else's problem we just "happened" to be connected somehow. It is in those times that we as God's people have a unique role to play. **"Blessed are the peacemakers, for they will be called sons of God." Matthew 5:9**

Howdy Stranger

The fact that Jesus commands us to initiate a conversation tells us a lot about the attitude that we are to have here on earth. **"And if you greet only your brothers, what are you doing more than others? Do not even the pagans do that?"** Mathew 5:47 Whether they are a friend, enemy, or stranger He would have us begin the interaction on His terms. If we are going to extend His Gospel and His love, it will have to begin with the greetings we extend to others.

"For the Son of Man came to seek and to save what was lost." Luke 19:10 Therefore, if anyone is in Christ, he is a new creation; the old has gone, the new has come! All this is from God, who reconciled us to himself through Christ and gave us the ministry of reconciliation: that God was reconciling the world to himself in Christ, not counting men's sins against them. And he has committed to us the message of reconciliation. We are therefore Christ's ambassadors, as though God were making his appeal through us. We implore you on Christ's behalf: Be reconciled to God. 2 Corinthians 5:17-20

First impressions are important. Often we won't get much of an opportunity to interact with people so what little time we may have needs to count. A good greeting goes a long way in making the minutes matter. It will also set the pace for the next encounter that you have with that person. It becomes a platform from which you can develop a relationship, share the Gospel, pass out a tract, or simply brighten someone's day.

As a part of our evangelistic work we take teams all over the world. Often we will end up living in the same community or area for a week or more. Our daily encounters with people, our greetings, (sometimes that's all we know in their language) helps set the stage for our effectiveness there, as we minister the Gospel. It will do the same thing wherever you are.

When it comes to our words we need a goal. We need Jesus' standard on this. **"For I do not speak of my own accord, but the Father who sent me commanded me what to say and how to say it." John 12:49**

Judge "Not"

Today in the United States we measure distance by the foot. The "foot" originated as the measurement of the king's foot in England. Unfortunately, each new king brought on a new measurement; and until it was standardized, it made parts of life very unstable. Go ahead and measure your foot. Most of us don't have a twelve-inch foot.

"Do not judge, and you will not be judged. Do not condemn, and you will not be condemned. Forgive, and you will be forgiven. Give, and it will be given to you. A good measure, pressed down, shaken together and running over, will be poured into your lap. For with the measure you use, it will be measured to you." Luke 6:37-38

How do we measure others? If it were up to us, we would all use a different measurement. Some of us would look for athletic achievements, or compassion, community contributions, educational achievements, financial success, or physical beauty. Once we had made our initial assessment then we might subtract or add points to a person as we learned more about them. In one person's eyes I could be a hero while in someone else's eyes I could be a waste of time. So how do we tell what is really going on?

"For all have sinned and fall short of the glory of God." Romans 3:23 God's measurement says we are all guilty. We are all equal. The achievements in athletics, good deeds, education, finances, or physical beauty don't change that. They may cloud our vision but they don't change what is really there. Each one of us is guilty before God. We all stand condemned already. So if we are guilty and condemned by God what do we really need? We need forgiveness. We need it from God and we need it from each other.

Love requires us to leave the condemnation and guilt to God. He is good at it and handles it in an appropriate way. We tend to twist it into a vindictive encounter. We can trash a person in ways God would never think of doing.

So do we forget the truth? No. **"Instead, speaking the truth in love, we will in all things grow up into him who is the Head, that is, Christ." Ephesians 4:15** When it is time and it is necessary, we need to speak the truth in love. But don't be too eager to speak. Find out what is really going on and then deal with it after you have God's approval on your actions. **"Stop judging by mere appearances, and make a right judgment." John 7:24**

When someone who lives on the streets gets saved it's true that they may need a bath, new clothes, and some goals in life. But love them first, rejoice with them first, and then offer to help them with all these great suggestions you have for their life. Nobody has the ministry of suggestion without the responsibility for action.

Our words can come from a heart that is filled with God's love and compassion or they can come from a heart filled with envy, bitterness, and strife. Whichever heart we have will determine how easy it is for us to **"judge not."** Keeping Christ's perspective on all this will allow us to function in a way that will draw those people we encounter closer to Him.

"If any one of you is without sin, let him be the first to throw a stone at her." John 8:7b

Look Ma! No Plank!

"You hypocrite, first take the plank out of your eye, and then you will see clearly to remove the speck from your brother's eye." Luke 6:42b There are certain sights, smells, and sounds that remind us of our past. They take us back every time we experience them. Unfortunately they can also make us very sensitive to the same things in others. We can assume too much about them based on our limited experience. We often end up pointing fingers at others because of our past.

When it came to sin Jesus called them hypocrites-those who point out other's sin while still practicing one form or another of it themselves. You can see why Jesus spoke so forcefully when you remember that His goal is love between God and people. He doesn't need us to hammer each other; he needs us to help.

So the first part of this command calls us to deal with the plank; repent, pull it out and replace it with one of Christ's commands. Once you have conquered the sin then you can share the path to victory with others. If you still have the plank, your best strategy is to ask the person with the speck how they got that far and then see if they would like to join you in seeking help for the speck that remains.

Too often we are afraid to associate with those who are struggling in the same area we are because it forces us to face the truth: we have a problem. It forces us all to be on the same level in life. Without a solid assurance of God's love for us we tend to put others down so that we can feel superior to someone.

Whenever we do this, we have forgotten some of the basic truths of life. All of us have sinned, all of us can know Father God because of Jesus, only Christ's blood can cleanse us, and we would all go to Hell if it weren't for God's love. Once we are in the family of God, we are all there by the grace and faith that He gives. None of us have a platform to stand on that makes us any higher than anyone else. There is no good, better, or best in the family of God. In fact, we are creating a real danger when we put people up on pedestals or push them down because of their past. We hide Jesus in the shadows that are created if we lift people up and admire them.

So when you see a murderer on trial, remember the last time you were angry with somebody and had murderous thoughts (Matthew 5:21-22). If a rapist is caught, remember the fantasy world you live in sometimes (Matthew 5:27-30). When you have removed those sins from your life then be willing to go to those who haven't and take the speck out of their eye.

You Flunked What?

For the next few years we will watch our kids work towards their driver's license. First they enroll in a special class. Then they get a permit that allows them to drive with a qualified driver in the car. Next they complete the class. Finally they take a written and driver's test. Once they have passed both tests, they are free to legally drive on our nation's roads.

Did you know they can flunk their final tests a hundred times and they can still come back and try again? In fact there is no limit to the amount of times they can try before they finally pass the test. Jesus tried to get that same point across to us when it comes to learning some of life's lessons.

Then Peter came to Jesus and asked, "Lord, how many times shall I forgive my brother when he sins against me? Up to seven times?" Jesus answered, "I tell you, not seven times, but seventy *times* seven times." Matthew 18:21-22

If we ever start keeping track of the times that others sin against us we will soon leave the road we are called to drive and sit in the bleachers staggering under the load of the lists we have kept. Those lists will become our lives. Those lists will become our stories. Those lists will become our legacy that we will pass on to our children. Those lists will keep us out of the Kingdom of God.

"**Therefore, the kingdom of heaven is like a king who wanted to settle accounts with his servants. As he began the settlement, a man who owed him ten thousand talents** [millions of dollars] **was brought to him. Since he was not able to pay, the master ordered that he and his wife and his children and all that he had be sold to repay the debt.**

"**The servant fell on his knees before him, 'Be patient with me,' he begged, 'and I will pay back everything.' The servant's master took pity on him, canceled the debt and let him go.**

"**But when that servant went out, he found one of his fellow servants who owed him a hundred denarii** [a few dollars]. **He grabbed him and began to choke him. 'Pay back what you owe me!' he demanded.**

"**His fellow servant fell to his knees and begged him, 'Be patient with me, and I will pay you back.'**

"**But he refused. Instead, he went off and had the man thrown into prison until he could pay the debt. When the other servants saw what had happened, they were greatly distressed and went and told their master everything that had happened.**

"**Then the master called the servant in. 'You wicked servant,' he said, 'I canceled all that debt of yours because you begged me to. Shouldn't you have had mercy on your fellow servant just as I had on you?' In anger his master turned him over to the jailers to be tortured, until he should pay back all he owed.**

"**This is how my heavenly Father will treat each of you unless you forgive your brother from your heart." Matthew 18:23-35**

Our forgiving is based on His forgiving first. He will forgive you for thousands of sins in your lifetime. You need to pass that forgiveness on to others. That will be easier for some because they recognize that when Jesus forgave them the first time, He forgave them for a multitude of sins. Others will appreciate what Jesus did but will not be as impressed. **"Therefore, I tell you, her many sins have been forgiven--for she loved much. But he who has been forgiven little loves little." Luke 7:47**

Sooner or later the only way we will be able to forgive others is because we have a daily time with our Heavenly Father where He loves and forgives us. In time we will all need to rely on that alone to forgive those who may sin against us dozens of times in a day.

Free from the lists, we will be able to run the race marked out for us. Foolish enough to fill out a list, we will find ourselves sidelined and reading the lists over and over and over again as the life Jesus has for us passes by. Forgive. Paint and repaint that line, daily.

People versus Possessions

"Give to everyone who asks you, and if anyone takes what belongs to you, do not demand it back. Do to others as you would have them do to you." Luke 6:30-31 "Give to the one who asks of you, and do not turn away from the one who wants to borrow from you." Matthew 5:42

Possessions and people don't always mix well. All over the world there is the struggle between those who don't have enough and those who do. People in power tend to hoard possessions at the expense of those who are starving at their gates. Here in the United States we have five percent of the world's population while we use a third of the world's resources. Just across our southern border, there are places where people die because they can't feed, clothe, or house their family properly. I've been there; I know.

We aren't supposed to be involved in the struggle; we are supposed to be involved in the solution. Loving people won't allow us to **"turn away"** from their plight when we can help. At that point our possessions become God's hand of help to those in need.

"I tell you, use worldly wealth to gain friends for yourselves, so that when it is gone, you will be welcomed into eternal dwellings." Luke 16:9 "Do not store up for yourselves treasures on earth, where moth

and rust destroy, and where thieves break in and steal. But store up for yourselves treasures in heaven, where moth and rust do not destroy, and where thieves do not break in and steal. For where your treasure is, there your heart will be also." Matthew 6:19-21

There are enough resources on the face of the earth so that no one has to go to bed hungry tonight. Unfortunately there aren't enough helping hands to feed them. There are enough resources so that no one has to be under-clothed. Unfortunately there aren't enough helping hands to clothe them. There are enough resources so that no one has to sleep without shelter. Unfortunately there aren't enough helping hands to build the structures.

When we use our resources in this way we properly represent the love of God to a dying world. At this point we have won the struggle in our own hearts-the struggle between possessions and people.

After this victory there is the next challenge. "So when you give to the needy, do not announce it with trumpets, as the hypocrites do in the synagogues and on the streets, to be honored by men. I tell you the truth, they have received their reward in full. But when you give to the needy, do not let your left hand know what your right hand is doing, so that your giving may be in secret. Then your Father, who sees what is done in secret, will reward you." Matthew 6:2-4 Pride pushes you out from between the two white lines and places you up in the stands so you can display your achievements. At that point you are going nowhere and doing no one any good.

You can see why Jesus asked us to hold our possessions in a giving posture. There are needs that only God's people will fill. There are traps along the way; that's why there are two white lines. If you are well-wrapped in God's love, you won't be tempted by pride as easily. If you know God's love, you won't just meet their material needs; you will meet the greater need as well; you will share the Gospel with them.

People and possessions will always be in competition for your emotions and energy. If you stay close to the first white line you will be able to define the second one. If you don't, you may end up in one of the many traps that are out there.

"The one who received the seed that fell among the thorns is the man who hears the word, but the worries of this life and the deceitfulness of wealth choke it, making it unfruitful." Matthew 13:22 The first white line will keep you from this trap; don't fear it. **Being confident of this, that he who began a good work in you will carry it on to completion until the day of Christ Jesus. Philippians 1:6**

People versus Position

You can't love people and positions at the same time. If you pursue positions, people will be hurt in the process. So Jesus took care of that for us with the commandments we are going to look at now.

Then James and John, the sons of Zebedee, came to him. "Teacher," they said, "we want you to do for us whatever we ask." Mark 10:35 They replied, "Let one of us sit at your right and the other at your left in your glory." Mark 10:37 When the ten heard about this, they became indignant [trouble always comes] with James and John. Jesus called them together and said, "You know that those who are regarded as rulers of the Gentiles lord it over them, and their high officials exercise authority over them. Not so with you. Instead, whoever wants to become great among you must be your servant, and whoever wants to be first must be slave of all. For even the Son of Man did not come to be served, but to serve, and to give his life as a ransom for many." Mark 10:41-45

Jesus modeled that all the way to the cross. He never lorded over any. He served and gave. In fact He had a following because they knew they could leave at anytime; sometimes they did (John 6:60-71). Jesus was a leader because He had followers who recognized that He had something to give to them, not get from them.

So how do people become leaders and fill those positions? They are picked based on the Godly characteristics they have displayed while serving. After the twelve were picked we see that the next set of leaders were picked as well (Acts 6:1-6). The books of Titus, and 1 and 2 Timothy have large sections devoted to picking future leaders. It is selection by those in authority, not promotion by one's self.

"When someone invites you to a wedding feast, do not take the place of honor, for a person more distinguished than you may have been invited. If so, the host who invited both of you will come and say to you, 'Give this man your seat.' Then, humiliated, you will have to take the least important place. But when you are invited, take the lowest place, so that when your host comes, he will say to you, 'Friend move up to a better place.' Then you will be honored in the presence of all your fellow guests. For everyone who exalts himself will be humbled, and he who humbles himself will be exalted." Luke 14:8-11.

Love God. Love people. Serve all. When invited, lead well. If you keep that priority, people will never become casualties because of positions. If you lose sight of that, the politically ugly messes that we see all over the world can become a part of the Church and its people.

Do Something

"Therefore, if you are offering your gift at the altar and there remember that your brother has something against you, leave your gift there in front of the altar. First go and be reconciled to your brother; then come and offer your gift.

"Settle matters quickly with your adversary who is taking you to court. Do it while you are still with him on the way, or he may hand you over to the judge, and the judge may hand you over to the officer, and you may be thrown into prison. I tell you the truth, you will not get out until you have paid the last penny." Matthew 5:23-26

"Be reconciled" and the word "quickly" stands out in these verses. Paul would encourage the same principle later when he said, "Make every effort to live in peace with all men ...." Hebrews 12:14a Strife divides. Within the body of Christ there is no place for division. We must "make every effort to live in peace with all men." Father God is so concerned about the body that He wants us to work out our problems among people before we come to Him with gifts.

If we don't then we are faced with some very unpleasant options. "See to it that no one misses the

grace of God and that no bitter root grows up to cause trouble and defile many." Hebrews 12:15 Left alone, people don't get better, they get bitter. Bitter people spill out the poison that has brewed inside and it infects others; trouble is soon to follow.

Trouble fragments the children in families (Colossians 3:21), separates the husband and wife (Matthew 19:6), and separates churches into a never-ending list of denominations and non-denominations. That spells TROUBLE and many are DEFILED.

If you find yourself thinking of individuals right now that are at odds with you, stop. **"Make every effort"** to **"reconcile, quickly."** If you find yourself without the words or means to do it then you can pray for help. **"If any of you lacks wisdom, he should ask God, who gives generously to all without finding fault, and it will be given to him." James 1:5**

If these scriptures touched you because you are bitter, you have three options. First, you can forgive. Often people are not even aware that they have hurt you. Second, you can forgive and then go and talk to the person if their behavior is sinful (not just inconvenient for you). **"If your brother sins against you, go and show him his fault, just between the two of you. If he listens to you, you have won your brother over. But if he will not listen, take one or two others along, so that 'every matter may be established by the testimony of two or three witnesses.' If he refuses to listen to them, tell it to the church; and if he refuses to listen even to the church, treat him as you would a pagan or a tax collector." Matthew 18:15-17**

Your third option is to stay bitter and get worse. You can't ignore the wound that caused the bitterness forever. It won't let you.

I shook the hand of an interesting man after church one night. It was an unusual shake because he was missing three fingers. When he told me his story it all went back to a little sliver that he got while working in his garage. He just didn't want to deal with it and it seemed so small. He developed blood poisoning, gangrene, and almost lost his arm. The three fingers were his sacrifice to the god of neglect. What you sacrifice to the god of bitterness could be much worse.

Since we have mentioned the passage in Matthew (18:15-17) that refers to church discipline, we also need to balance it with the passage from Galatians (6:1-2) that covers another setting for sin and a brother. **"Brothers, if someone is caught in a sin, you who are spiritual should restore him gently. But watch yourself, or you also may be tempted. Carry each other's burdens, and in this way you will fulfill the law of Christ." Galatians 6:1-2**

God's ultimate goal is that we be reconciled one to another despite who we are and what we do. Then we can enjoy the fullness of our relationship with our Heavenly Father. That always requires work on our part. So get good at it. You will find miles of smooth travel down the highway if this section is well painted.

When Things Don't Change

"Blessed are you when people insult you, persecute you and falsely say all kinds of evil against you because of me. Rejoice and be glad, because great is your reward in heaven, for in the same way they persecuted the prophets who were before you." Matthew 5:11-12

Christians receive a variety of treatment all over the world. In some places they are in power politically and respected. In other places their Christian faith makes them criminals. Whatever you face **"because of"** Christ, be blessed. Apparently you made enough of an impact with your faith that some people were uncomfortable.

This doesn't mean that you can be an idiot in your actions and then be blessed by the way you are treated. Titus had to work with those kinds of "Christians" in Crete. **"They claim to know God, but by their actions they deny him. They are detestable, disobedient and unfit for doing anything good." Titus 1:16**

Our obedience to Christ's commands sets a standard that can make others look bad. Sometimes that means trouble for us. Our obedience to Christ's personal direction will determine whether that trouble is just a "blessing," the preliminary steps of a martyr, or a call to move on.

"When you are persecuted in one place, flee to another. I tell you the truth, you will not finish going through the cities of Israel before the Son of Man comes." Matthew 10:23 "If anyone will not welcome you or listen to your words, shake the dust off your feet when you leave that home or town." Matthew 10:14

If Christ has called you to a place to make your stand for Him then trouble can escalate into hostility against you. Jesus felt the full brunt of that hostility as He made His stand in Israel. Jesus could have left. But Jesus didn't leave because He was called to a specific place and people.

Jesus gave the commands we just read to His disciples because they weren't called to the same ministry. History tells us that most of the disciples died outside of Israel. They died in places they were called to or got caught in. Paul left many hostile situations (read the book of Acts). When He left, the local Christians stayed behind. Whether you stay or leave will depend on your personal calling in life.

Currently I serve Christ as an evangelist. That can be done anywhere in the world. If persecution began to prevent me from obeying Christ in one area, I would be free to move on, not to be quiet. I have served Christ as a pastor. At that point I would be called to stay unless I was given specific direction otherwise. That direction might include moving the whole body of believers elsewhere.

Whatever situation you become a part of, don't let the persecution surprise you or stop you from obeying what Christ has called you to. People who obey Christ are a part of the fiber that holds any country together. We are not to expect perfect treatment from others because of it. Christians are persecuted worldwide. You live in the same world they do so don't be surprised by what may happen to you.

"All this I have told you so that you will not go astray. They will put you out of the synagogue; in fact, a time is coming when anyone who kills you will think he is offering a service to God. They will do such things because they have not known the Father or me." John 16:1-3

The Heart Monitor

"Again, you have heard that it was said to the people long ago, 'Do not break your oath, but keep the oaths you have made to the Lord.' But I tell you, Do not swear at all: either by heaven, for it is God's throne; or by the earth, for it is his footstool; or by Jerusalem, for it is the city of the Great King. And do not swear by your head, for you cannot make even one hair white or black. Simply let your 'Yes' be 'Yes,' and your 'No,' 'No'; anything beyond this comes from the evil one." Matthew 5:33-37

We try to hide behind our words. It isn't much of a disguise but we seem to try it anyway. If we are afraid, we cover up. If we have been lazy or forgotten a promise, we can buy a little more time if we cover up with our words; that way we won't look bad. If someone questions our statements, we raise our lies to a new level and can even swear on a stack of Bibles. All this lying on our part only delays our lessons about real life and ourselves. Even more importantly it shows us what is really going on in our hearts. You see, your mouth is your heart monitor.

"Make a tree good and its fruit will be good, or make a tree bad and its fruit will be bad, for a tree is recognized by its fruit. You brood of vipers, how can you who are evil say anything good? *For out of the overflow of the heart the mouth speaks.* The good man brings good things out of the good stored up in him, and the evil man brings evil things out of the evil stored up in him. But I tell you that men will have to give account on the day of judgment for every careless word they have spoken. For by your words you will be acquitted, and by your words you will be condemned." Matthew 12:33-37 (Italics mine)

We must spend time loving God and letting God love us or our hearts won't have an overflow of His love for others. It shows up first in our words. Are we afraid? Do we fear punishment? There is no fear in love. But perfect love drives out fear, because fear has to do with punishment. The one who fears is not made perfect in love. 1 John 4:18 Do we hurt? Are we in trouble? Our words will betray us.

Praise be to the God and Father of our Lord Jesus Christ, the Father of compassion and the God of all comfort, who comforts us in all our troubles, so that we can comfort those in any trouble with the comfort we ourselves have received from God. 2 Corinthians 1:3-4 Are we avoiding the truth about others or ourselves? Are we protecting an image? We don't need to wear masks with God nor each other.

No discipline seems pleasant at the time, but painful. Later on, however, it produces a harvest of righteousness and peace for those who have been trained by it. Hebrews 12:11

All these show us what is or isn't inside. Don't be afraid of it; God isn't. He is big enough to deal with who you really are today so that you can become what you were intended to be tomorrow. In all my prayers for all of you, I always pray with joy because of your partnership in the gospel from the first day until now, being

confident of this, that he who began a good work in you will carry it on to completion until the day of Christ Jesus. Philippians 1:4-6

A heart full of the love of God can say 'Yes,' and 'No,' and live with the consequences that follow. A heart that isn't full of His love will try to hide behind a wall of words or oaths. Pay attention to the monitor. Respond immediately when it emits a warning sign. Your physical life depends on your heart; it isn't any different in your spiritual life.

Mission Field or Missionary

"But woe to you who are rich, for you have already received your comfort. Woe to you who are well fed now, for you will go hungry. Woe to you who laugh now, for you will mourn and weep. Woe to you when all men speak well of you, for that is how their fathers treated the false prophets." Luke 6:24-26

I have ministered in several countries where Buddhism has a strong influence. One of the outcomes of those teachings is that suffering is only addressed in teaching, not action. Buddists believe people suffer in life because they did something in a past life to merit the current suffering. That means you let someone lie in the street if they were hit by a car; after all they did something before to deserve it. As heartless as that is it isn't much different than the United States where people starve to death, crime victims lie in the street, or children go home to cook for themselves and fall asleep watching TV.

Jesus was addressing those who did not participate in the problems of humanity. They had the resources and they were alive, but they used their time and life for their own pursuits. You could get the essence of Christ's words with a similar statement. *Woe to you who are a part of the problem and not the solution. Woe to you who are a part of the status quo and not doing anything for change. Woe to you who are still a part of the mission field when you could be a missionary.*

As you begin to live within the two white lines you will notice that you are more involved in people's lives. Many of these lives will be fractured. Many of those lives will not know Jesus Christ as Savior and Lord. You will become one of their links to Father God. In one respect you become His hand extended to them. As long as you stay within those lines you will have the strength to minister and you will see the need to minister (a potential opportunity).

Jesus faced a culture that had all the problems that humanity could generate. There was crime of every kind. Slavery was normal. Lepers and cripples were not treated as complete people. In all of this the religious community had created rules to excuse themselves from dealing with these issues. "Sin" was always the cause for a rough time in life so they could avoid those people. In fact they had created enough rules that they did not have to deal with much of anything or anyone. If life was going well for them it was obviously God's "blessings," so they could live as they saw fit.

Today there are enough resources in the world to feed and properly clothe everyone. Many diseases are preventable by readily available vaccines. Pennies a day will educate people in the basic skills of reading and writing. Travel and communication tools have never been cheaper and more readily available. Christians could spread the Gospel worldwide, feed and clothe all they meet, and teach them the basics of education for life in a matter of years--if we would allow God to mold our hearts to the following commands of Christ.

Looking at his disciples, he said: "Blessed are you who are poor, for yours is the kingdom of God. Blessed are you who hunger now, for you will be satisfied. Blessed are you who weep now, for you will laugh. Blessed are you when men hate you, when they exclude you and insult you and reject your name as evil, because of the Son of Man. Rejoice in that day and leap for joy, because great is your reward in heaven. For that is how their fathers treated the prophets." Luke 6:20-23

They were **"poor"** because they gave all they had to meet the needs they saw; they weren't lazy. They were **"hungry"** because they saw a need and they didn't have time to eat; it wasn't that they couldn't hold down a job. They **"wept"** as they saw what was really out there. Others **"hated"** them because they saw their own selfishness and sin in the mirror of the prophets' faces. Prophets were treated poorly because they tried to treat everyone with the truth from God. In other words, *blessed are those who participate in what is really going on as God's hands and heart extend into a world that is dying without Him.*

When you have traveled between the two white lines for any length of time you will find that there are people on the road who need what you have learned. As you begin to share what you have with them you step into a world called "ministry." If you seem drawn to those already on the track then you probably have a calling from God to help strengthen the church. If you seem to cry most for those not yet on the road then your heart may be molded for missions or evangelistic work.

Some people are called ministers because of education, but Jesus would like to call us "ministers" because it describes our actions. Living between the two white lines will build that into us. Our obedience creates a well that we draw from to help others. The remaining commands that Jesus left for us are based on the assumption that we have already applied the basic commands, the commands we have already looked at. If those are a growing part of our lives, we can apply the ministry commands and become *God's hands and heart* to those in need. Our experience between the two white lines are the resources we draw from. The more we have, the more we can give to those in need.

"MINISTRY"
The
by-product
of your time
between the
two white
lines.

Follow Me

Everyone that follows Jesus will be asked to put His commands into practice. That is what makes us alike. These commands will make it possible for us to get along and work together all over the world. But as soon as we have all gone through our spiritual boot camp, He will start to work at making us very different.

Jesus answered, "If I want him to remain alive until I return, what is that to you? You must follow me." John 21:22 Peter had just heard that he would die an uncomfortable death (John 21:18-19). His initial reaction was to ask about John, what would happen to him? Jesus gave the reply that we all need to hear, **"You must follow me."** After the basics, Jesus doesn't send us out on our own. We are always to live in-between the two white lines. Where we do that and what we go through in our obedience will vary greatly; but it will always be dependent on our obedience to the specific places and people that Jesus directs us towards.

In the Gospels the phrase **"follow me"** is common. You will never find Jesus asking for a vote on a decision. You will never find Jesus flipping a coin. Instead Jesus was in constant contact with Father God and all of His actions reflected God's guidance, **"but the world must**

learn that I love the Father and that I do exactly what my Father has commanded me. Come now; let us leave." John 14:31

What type of ministry we are ultimately involved in will be dependent on Jesus' desires and plans for us. You can't look at someone else and determine your future. Though you learned to put Jesus' commands into practice along with everyone else, at some point your obedience to Jesus' commands will set you apart. Jesus won't desert you but you won't have the same experience as others; only you, Jesus, and a few close people will really understand and share your life.

Some people will have an international ministry and be well known and respected by millions of people (Billy Graham). Others will labor unnoticed in a sixth grade Sunday School class. If each is walking in obedience to Jesus, **"what is that to you?"** This really means something if you happen to be with the sixth graders. Yet no matter where and who you minister to, you will find that you have a shrinking circle of friends who understand. Fortunately, Jesus is always in the center of that circle.

The Message

From that time on Jesus began to preach, "Repent, for the kingdom of heaven is near." Matthew 4:17 It is the message that you responded to, it is the only message that leaves room for all that Jesus intends to do; so preach, teach, speak, live repentance. When people saw the change in you they knew something had happened. Unless people repent there is no hope for them to see the impact of the Gospel in their lives. Where will God build an understanding of real love, forgiveness, hope, holiness, power, and purity unless they have repented and have made room for it?

This is not a popular message. You will not always be appreciated for it. For when you preach it you are saying that the way people are living is wrong. Painting a house a different color is one thing. Tearing it down, hauling off the rubble, and building a completely new one that is a different color is another matter.

Straying from this message will diminish the results in a person's life and the chance they have to learn to live between the two white lines. Every fruitful minister has learned to live and preach this message.

Peter replied, "Repent and be baptized, every one of you, in the name of Jesus Christ for the forgiveness

of your sins. And you will receive the gift of the Holy Spirit." Acts 2:38 "In the past God overlooked such ignorance, but now he commands all people everywhere to repent." Acts 17:30 (Paul)

The Pace-Love the Children

People were bringing little children to Jesus to have him touch them, but the disciples rebuked them. When Jesus saw this, he was indignant. He said to them, "Let the little children come to me, and do not hinder them, for the kingdom of God belongs to such as these. Mark 10:13-14

Looking out over an inner city street scene you see why Jesus said, **"do not hinder them (the children) from coming to me."** Once the pain and poverty of life is etched into people's hearts they don't respond as easily to the help that Jesus and His people offer. Babies and small children have an inherent appeal; teenagers don't. Angry, bitter, and socially disfigured teenagers scare most people.

God's original basic design for children makes sense. Give the parent's months to prepare for the birth, years to love and bond with a "cute kid," and then when they are not as easy to love, rely on what has been built over the years to carry them through the tough times.

Unfortunately for kids and our society, that plan is seldom followed any more. Single parents who have to work, unwed mothers who treat the baby as a living doll, parents who despise the inconvenience that a new baby brings, have all helped to bring about a generation of teens that scares the rest of society. Normal homes are not without blame either as parents have spent their time pursuing careers and cash. That has left a vacuum in the home that many teens have tried to fill with drugs, sex, and illicit thrills.

All of us who have had kids of our own should be children's ministers. If you have raised them past the ages of ten then you have some experience in youth ministry. Those of you who have witnessed your children mature to the point of marriage could write a chapter in a young adult ministry manual. All this life experience should be shared with others. God didn't get us through those years with ours so we could sit on the sidelines and criticize others who are still in the middle of it. If we didn't do so well with ours then we could spare others some of the painful lessons we have faced.

"And whoever welcomes a little child like this in my name welcomes me. But if anyone causes one of these little ones who believe in me to sin, it would be better for him to have a large millstone hung around his neck and to be drowned in the depths of the sea." Matthew 18:5-6

Somehow parents seem to have this concept built into their hearts. Even if they aren't going to church and they have no intention of going themselves, they will bring their kids or let a neighbor do it. There are exceptions but God's warning seems to have been heard.

It also shows us just what the limiting factor should be in our society: children. We should keep a pace in life that allows children to flourish. Instead we set our pace by our bank account, recreational interests, or dreams and desires. That pace puts stumbling blocks in front of kids all the time. "They didn't have time for me, she was always at church, the TV raised me, they never came to my event."

All these are stumbling blocks that become problems in the teenage years.

"See that you do not look down on one of these little ones. For I tell you that their angels in heaven always see the face of my Father in heaven." Matthew **18:10** Keeping the kid pace will include loving the unlovely. Deformities, injuries, mental capacities, big ears, a never-ending mouth, or a unique marking can place kids on the low end of a "cuteness scale." Love them. Don't keep a "cuteness scale" around. Then transfer that attitude to everyone you see.

Having children as our pacemakers will make the journey between the two white lines complete. We will have time to smell the roses because we know the children will stop to pick them. Any society that keeps this pace will be self-perpetuating and strong. If we don't keep this pace, we must be ready for the stern judgment that Jesus promised.

Clothed With Power

"**I am going to send you what my Father has promised; but stay in the city until you have been clothed with power from on high.**" **Luke 24:49** The disciples did just that. After days of waiting they received the power (as is recorded in Acts chapter two). With it Peter preached his first sermon and saw three thousand people begin to follow Jesus (Acts 2:41). That represents power.

Unlike some events in life which only happen once, this event was repeated again in Acts 4:31. In fact, you will see it repeated every time people needed to be introduced to or reinforced by the power that our Father in Heaven had promised (Acts 8:14-19, Acts 10, Acts 19:1-10). Living with that power is a prerequisite to fulfilling the ministry that Jesus will direct you into. Waiting for that power is another prerequisite.

This is not a new biblical principle. Like so many of the Old Testament truths, Jesus had to bring them out again and with their proper meaning. **Even youths grow tired and weary, and young men stumble and fall; but those who hope [***wait,*** KJV] in the Lord will renew their strength. They will soar on wings like eagles; they will**

run and not grow weary, they will walk and not be faint. Isaiah 40:30-31.

"Hope (NIV)" or "wait (KJV)" means to become intertwined. If, you try to pull a car out of the ditch with kite string you are guaranteed to fail. If, however, you take that string and intertwine it with a two-inch dock rope you will succeed. When you wait as commanded and as needed, you will have the strength to face the challenge. Any portable tool needs to have its batteries recharged; you are no different. That means you are still dependent on the one who gives the power. Staying between the two white lines will make the power necessary but also available. Your ministry will be carried with this power or wither without it.

Waiting is not something we always do very well. But when we consider who we are waiting with and for, it will take on a whole new dimension. This will be another factor we must consider as we establish a pace of ministry for our lives. We must plan for, cherish, and guard our time in God's wait (weight) room. Only with that discipline built into our lives can we maintain and increase our spiritual strength.

Get Ready

"That servant who knows his master's will and does not get ready or does not do what his master wants will be beaten with many blows." Luke 12:47 His plans for us are important. His plans for us affect people all over the world. Our response to His plans should be obedience or preparation. When we are obedient, the love of Christ is extended through us. We accomplish the heart-cry of God wherever we go.

Anything big requires planning and preparation. Some things require a lifetime of planning and preparation. Some of the tasks that Jesus calls us to will have required years of experience, training, and maturing. Some will prepare for it and be ready; others will hear the call and not do enough to get ready for it. **"For many are invited, but few are chosen." Matthew 22:14.**

Statistics show that less than twenty percent of those who enter a full-time ministry vocation will remain in that vocation for five years. Eighty percent were not ready for the realities of ministry; they were not prepared for what they faced. Called by God? Yes. Properly prepared? No. They didn't have enough time between the two white lines or didn't stay there once they entered into full-time ministry.

172

Looking at those that make it through the first five years of ministry, eighty percent of them will be in full-time ministry until the day they retire or die (whichever comes first). They had enough experience between the two lines and continued to live there throughout their lifetime. It isn't complicated. It just requires a practical application of Christ's commands on a daily basis. That keeps you between the two white lines.

If things stop working we need to examine the basic areas of our lives. Jesus gave us some very practical ways to check. **"I am the vine; you are the branches. If a man remains in me and I in him, he will bear much fruit; apart from me you can do nothing." John 15:5** If your hand doesn't lift when you tell it to with your mind, you automatically know that something is wrong. You make an appointment with the doctor. If it is a spiritual part of your life you need to make an appointment with Jesus.

In the body of Christ we see the result of that all the time. We know God's will and we don't do it. Something is wrong. It can be a lot of things. Maybe we just don't like that order from God. Perhaps we are afraid of failing. Some just didn't get ready and now that the time has come, they couldn't do it if they wanted to. Others are fruitless because the cares and worries of this life have sapped their energy and enthusiasm. All of these explanations fit under the title of sin. And with all sin there is a death to something **(For the wages of sin is death, but the gift of God is eternal life in Christ Jesus our Lord. Romans 6:23)**. No matter what our society says about sin, what the Bible says still holds true.

Following Jesus will guarantee tough assignments. There will be times when you don't understand, agree with, or desire to do what "Lord" Jesus is asking you to do. In those times He is definitely "Lord" Jesus. In those times will you be His servant and work towards accomplishing His will?

Looking back over the tough assignments you will see the why of it and appreciate the result of it even if you dreaded every minute of it. Those times will humble you and cause you once again to see your place on the road and why there are two white lines to guide you on it. If you aren't ready for the assignment or you rebel against it you may see something as a result of your action--things that no one was ever meant to see. **"They have built the high places of Baal to burn their sons in the fire as offerings to Baal--something I did not command or mention, nor did it enter my mind. So beware, the days are coming, declares the Lord, when people will no longer call this place Topheth or the Valley of Ben Hinnom, but the Valley of Slaughter." Jeremiah 19:5-6.**

Extreme? Yes. Historical? Unfortunately. Write a history that is based on obedience.

Go!

He told them, "The harvest is plentiful, but the workers are few. Ask the Lord of the harvest, therefore, to send out workers into his harvest field. Go! I am sending you out like lambs among wolves." Luke 10:2-3 "As you go preach this message: 'The kingdom of heaven is near.' Heal the sick, raise the dead, cleanse those who have leprosy, drive out demons. Freely you have received, freely give." Matthew 10:7-8

Right now there are people praying that you will go. They are praying for people to come to their country to tell them about "this Jesus they have heard of and the great book from heaven." Others are praying for someone to talk to a relative who won't listen to them. At some point in our lives we will be called past our circle of friends and surroundings to go. That isn't always easy for us to accept or act on but the call will come.

When we go we already have our agenda. We are to preach Christ's message and do Christ's works. As with all of Christ's commands, this one will take awhile to master. We will still live between the two white lines; we will just be there outside of familiar surroundings. Maturity will mean that we see new stretches of the Autobahn.

It may start with a neighbor across the fence before it becomes a country across the sea. Your first experience may be with a short-term mission trip or a vacation where you suddenly see a need. Your job may take you there the first time but Jesus will lead you back. Be ready to go, don't be afraid of it, and when you do go, know that everything you have learned up to this point still applies.

Your time in the harvest field will be a time to expand your first-hand knowledge and understanding of your Lord Jesus and our Father in Heaven. Most of the New Testament occurrences took place outside of the synagogue. For many people most of their Christian experience happens in a church. When you offer yourself to the harvest you will begin to see things happen anywhere Jesus leads you. As you grow with each one of these experiences, you will have that much more to pass on to others.

Go! I can't predict what is out there for you. But I can predict who will be there with you. Go, despite your doubts.

Then the eleven disciples went to Galilee, to the mountain where Jesus had told them to go. When they saw him, they worshipped him; but some doubted. Then Jesus came to them and said, "All authority in heaven and on earth has been given to me. Therefore go and make disciples of all nations, baptizing them in the name of the Father and of the Son and of the Holy Spirit, and teaching them to obey everything I have commanded you. And surely I am with you always, to the very end of the age." Matthew 28:16-20

Greater Things

"I tell you the truth, anyone who has faith in me will do what I have been doing. He will do even greater things than these, because I am going to the Father." John 14:12 We are therefore Christ's ambassadors, as though God were making his appeal through us. We implore you on Christ's behalf: Be reconciled to God. 2 Corinthians 5:20

As you go, you will learn to go as an ambassador with the heart and all the power of the Kingdom you represent. This learning experience will take many lessons and many miles between the two white lines before you are comfortable working in this realm. Like the first disciples, we all have a lot to learn in this new realm of power and love.

When the disciples James and John saw this, they asked, "Lord, do you want us to call fire down from heaven to destroy them?" But Jesus turned and rebuked them, and they went to another village. Luke 9:54-56 Possible? Yes! The will of God? No! Jesus rebuked them because they had started to recognize the power possibilities but didn't have the heart to apply it properly. After some more instruction Jesus sent them out to work in the power realm again (Luke 10:1-16). Their return tells us something more about the realm of power that we can work in.

The seventy-two returned with joy and said, "Lord, even the demons submit to us in your name." He replied, "I saw Satan fall like lighting from heaven. I have given you authority to trample on snakes and scorpions and to overcome all the power of the enemy; nothing will harm you. However, do not rejoice that the spirits submit to you, but rejoice that your names are written in heaven." Luke 10:17-20

Power corrupts and absolute power can corrupt absolutely. That saying has a lot of truth to it. Jesus wants us to avoid that pitfall by remembering that He died so we could live as His ambassadors in His power with His heart. Without the heart, the power takes on a twisted place in the religious community with bizarre manifestations.

Some Jews who went around driving out evil spirits tried to invoke the name of the Lord Jesus over those who were demon-possessed. They would say, "In the name of Jesus, whom Paul preaches, I command you to come out." Seven sons of Sceva, a Jewish chief priest, were doing this. One day the evil spirit answered them, "Jesus I know, and I know about Paul, but who are you?" Then the man who had the evil spirit jumped on them and overpowered them all. He gave them such a beating they ran out of the house naked and bleeding. Acts 19:13-16

Only the two white lines will keep us out of that kind of trouble. Loving God and the people in our world will enable us to learn what to do in the limitless situations we may encounter. We will begin to understand even more of Christ's life and His dependency on our Heavenly Father. **Jesus gave them this answer: "I tell you the truth, the Son can do nothing by himself; he can do only what he** sees his Father doing, because whatever the Father does the Son also does. **John 5:19**

Doing His works, His way, with His heart, will require the same dependency He had as He walked between the two white lines. **Heal the sick, raise the dead, cleanse those who have leprosy, drive out demons. Freely you have received, freely give. Matthew 10:8**

Guess Who's Coming to Dinner?

Then Jesus said to his host, "When you give a luncheon or dinner, do not invite your friends, your brothers or relatives, or your rich neighbors; if you do, they may invite you back and so you will be repaid. But when you give a banquet, invite the poor, the crippled, the lame, the blind, and you will be blessed. Although they cannot repay you, you will be repaid at the resurrection of the righteous." Luke 14:12-14

At some point in your ministry you can end up spending all your time ministering to Christ's followers. At times like that Jesus will remind you that you are also called as Jesus was to the lost **(For the Son of Man came to seek and to save what was lost. Luke 19:10).** Reaching out to those who can't reach back is a trademark of the love of God. Feeding those less fortunate than you is a tangible way to express that love.

As each of us travels between the two white lines we may find ourselves becoming more specialized in what we do. Some will work with children. Others will provide hands and skills wherever they are needed in the church. A few will end up as vocational pastors, teachers, prophets, apostles, and evangelists.

Others will have the same gifts but will work a full time job and volunteer within the church. Their ministry will be split between the church and the places where they work. Their paying job may enable them to minister in areas where there is no financial support or there are religious restrictions for Christian workers.

Foreign countries will receive those who end up as missionaries. In all these gifts (Ephesians 4:11, Romans 12:3-8, 1 Corinthians 12) only a few are focused on reaching the lost. Even those with the evangelistic focus can lose sight of that purpose if they become bogged down with the details of their work.

This verse reminds us who we are called to reach and gives us one way to do it. Many churches and Christians have become consumed with the details of life and have forgotten the two white lines that are there to guide us. Loving the unloved will force us to cling closely to the first white line. That will enable us to bring those unloved into the company of the **"beloved."** Deuteronomy 33:12

Awkward? Potentially. This group of people just might refuse your invitation. Ungrateful? Possibly. You might not get thanked at all. Love isn't always easy. Obedient? Yes. You will have extended Christ's hand of love in a tangible way. Only time will tell how the human recipients will respond. But Christ will be blessed immediately by the labor of His co-workers.

Made for Miracles

As evening approached, the disciples came to him and said, "This is a remote place, and it's already getting late. Send the crowds away, so they can go to the villages and buy themselves some food.

Jesus replied, "They do not need to go away. You give them something to eat."

"We have here only five loaves of bread and two fish," they answered.

"Bring them here to me," he said. And he directed the people to sit down on the grass. Taking the five loaves and the two fish and looking up to heaven, he gave thanks and broke the loaves. Then he gave them to the disciples, and the disciples gave them to the people. They all ate and were satisfied, and the disciples picked up twelve basketfuls of broken pieces that were left over. The number of those who ate was about five thousand men, besides women and children. Matthew 14:15-21

Life is custom-made for miracles. It is full of settings and situations where a miracle would ... well, it would make life easier, prevent some disaster, correct a wrong, or alleviate some suffering. The stage for a miracle is set more often than the number of times one shows up. So we continue to see the heartache, evil, and suffering when we think a miracle could have, should have, shown up. Why? Why not a miracle?

Jesus said to them, "Only in his hometown, among his relatives and in his own house is a prophet without honor." He could not do any miracles there, except lay his hands on a few sick people and heal them. And he was amazed at their lack of faith. Mark 6:4-6

Jesus was there. The needs were there. And **"he could not do any miracles there."** People must participate with God in the working of miracles and do so on His terms.

"The time came when the beggar died and the angels carried him to Abraham's side. The rich man also died and was buried. In hell, where he was in torment, he looked up and saw Abraham far away, with Lazarus by his side. So he called to him, 'Father Abraham, have pity on me and send Lazarus to dip the tip of his finger in water and cool my tongue, because I am in agony in this fire.'

"But Abraham replied, 'Son, remember that in your lifetime you received your good things, while Lazarus received bad things, but now he is comforted here and you are in agony. And besides all this, between us and you a great chasm has been fixed, so that those who want to go from here to you cannot, nor can anyone cross over from there to us.' Luke 16:22-26

Some suffering will continue because the judgment of God is taking place. God's holiness will not be compromised for our convenience. He is not here to serve us; rather we are here to serve Him. So you won't find miracles happening when they would cross the lines of what is right in the sight of God.

As you can see, miracles will always live between the tension of what we want, what we have the faith for, and what is right before God. After you have traveled between the two white lines for a while you will realize that miracles need to be initiated and confirmed by God. Hebrews chapter eleven gives us that long list of Old Testament heroes who heard the miracles message from God and acted on it. It is no different for us.

Hug the first white line for miracles. Hear God's heart and wisdom for that situation. Understand the real issues involved. Miracles will come. In fact it is one of the trademarks of the kind of believers that Jesus will be building with this commandment that he left for us. **"Believe me when I say that I am in the Father and the Father is in me; or at least believe on the evidence of the miracles themselves. I tell you the truth, anyone who has faith in me will do what I have been doing. He will do even greater things that these, because I am going to the Father." John 14:11-12**

Rest

Then, because so many people were coming and going that they did not even have a chance to eat, he said to them, "Come with me by yourselves to a quiet place and get some rest." Mark 6:31

The needs of people in this world are endless. Those who have walked between the two white lines for any length of time will begin to see those needs and become a part of meeting them; but only a part. To stay a healthy, whole, useful part of the solution you have to find a way to keep the three ingredients mentioned in this verse in your life.

"With me." Time with Jesus, the first white line, can be easily crowded out. Ministry demands can keep you up late, force you to skip meals, and squeeze every drop of strength right out of you. It can also fill every hour of your day with "critical needs" and "projects." Jesus flourished in His ministry here because He was consistently heading off into the hills somewhere to pray by Himself. You can't replace time alone with Jesus with anything else.

"A quiet place." Distractions detract from our time with Jesus. Someone who is constantly ministering (as the disciples were at this point) needs to know silence again. It is in that silence that the peace and the power come by the Holy Spirit. When we are empowered and guided by the Holy Spirit our efforts towards the needs of this world go twice as far and impact individuals ten times as much. The details of ministry are accomplished because our timing is right and we are working with God on His projects, not stumbling around in a frenzy just trying to do something. If we have enough time in the quiet places we can face the most frantic scene with the peace and confidence that only the Holy Spirit can bring.

"Rest" is a four-letter word for some people. They have confused it with another four-letter word, "lazy." If you are lazy, you don't do what you could do. If you don't rest, you can't do what you should do. We still have mortal bodies. Our new bodies are a future experience in Heaven. Until that time we can live a supernatural life because we **"Come with me by yourselves to a quiet place and get some rest."** Being in the right place, at the right time, with the right things to say and do are only possible with regular times of rest.

We are commanded to rest on the seventh day. For people in ministry, that isn't always easy. Their seventh day can be one of the busiest. So they will need to find their own seventh day and their own daily time of refreshing. Without it, the other six days will not hold enough hours to finish the work God has for them.

"Listen"

Jesus turned and said to Peter, "Get behind me, Satan! You are a stumbling block to me; you do not have in mind the things of God, but the things of men." Matthew 16:23
When we are wrong Jesus will tell us.   Listen. Respond without any excuses, pride, or fear.   People seldom understand all that is going on in life.   Our eyes rarely see all the circumstances behind someone's actions. Jesus does see and understand.   When He needs to rebuke you, He will.   For those in ministry situations it is critical that we set aside time to listen.   If we are in error we need to know because our mistakes don't stop with us.

Not many of you should presume to be teachers, my brothers, because you know that we who teach will be judged more strictly.   James 3:1 Your ministry to others becomes seeds in their lives, seeds that can grow into maturity or deformity.   God's work, done God's way, produces godly results.   God's work, attempted in our time, with our words, and our understanding, has produced a divided, embittered, uncoordinated, religious community. People will be judged for the part they have played in producing the mess we now live with.

In the book of Revelation, Jesus takes all of chapters two and three to rebuke the churches that John had been ministering in. As you read the rebukes you will notice that they are very direct and pointed. Names are mentioned. As Jesus finishes, He leaves them with the same encouragement that we can look forward to.

"Those whom I love I rebuke and discipline. So be earnest, and repent. Here I am! I stand at the door and knock. If anyone hears my voice and opens the door, I will come in and eat with him, and he with me. To him who overcomes, I will give the right to sit with me on my throne, just as I overcame and sat down with my Father on his throne. He who has an ear, let him hear what the Spirit says to the churches." Revelation 3:19-22

Listen. He will speak if He needs to.

Bottom of the 9th

I took my whole family to the last game of the season for our local professional baseball team. It wasn't very impressive. They didn't start all the regulars. And when the team fell way behind in the fifth inning, a lot of people got up and left. They wanted to see them win or see the regulars break some more records. We stayed till the, alas, "bitter end."

We watched as they "almost" pulled off an incredible comeback. With a team full of names I had never heard of before they "almost" won the game. It was the bottom of the ninth, two out, two strikes, and the winning runs were on base. They had scored a lot of runs to get this close. Why not just a few more.

One day as Jesus was standing by the Lake of Gennesaret, with the people crowding around him and listening to the word of God, he saw at the water's edge two boats, left there by the fisherman, who were washing their nets [that's what you do every day when you are done fishing]. **He got into one of the boats, the one belonging to Simon, and asked him to put out a little from shore. Then he sat down and taught the people from the boat.**

When he had finished speaking, he said to Simon, "Put out into deep water, and let down the nets for a catch."

Simon answered, "Master, we've worked hard all night and haven't caught anything. But because you say so, I will let down the nets [the ones they had just finished washing]. When they had done so, they caught such a large number of fish that their nets began to break. So they signaled their partners in the other boat to come and help them, and they came and filled both boats so full that they began to sink.

When Simon Peter saw this, he fell at Jesus' knees and said, "Go away from me, Lord; I am a sinful man!" Luke 5:1-8

Bottom of the ninth, two out, two strikes, and the next guy up hits a grand slam home run off the best relief pitcher in the league. The crowd (those that stayed) goes wild. History is made. Will you be a part of History, or will you be in the parking lot fighting traffic trying to get home?

Until you're dead, you're not done. Peter thought the day was over. And only out of obedience to Jesus did he put those nets down one more time, the nets that he had just cleaned and put away. Only obedience to the words of Jesus enabled Peter to see the biggest catch possible; a catch that almost sank his boat, a catch that brought Peter to his knees. Yes, Peter was a fisherman. Yes, Peter knew the sea. Yes, Peter had given up.

Don't leave the stadium until it's over. Don't stop what Jesus has called you to do until He says you're done. Don't quit what you're doing just because it doesn't seem to be working. If Jesus called you to it, don't quit. I know a missionary who worked for twelve years before he saw the first native begin to follow Jesus. He had washed his nets thousands of times knowing that nothing had been caught. Back home his brother was the pastor of a church with thousands of people attending on a Sunday. Wanted to quit? I'm sure. Asked to quit? Yes. Encouraged to do something else? Often.

Twelve years after he cast the net the first time he caught one fish. There would be more. In fact nearly the whole tribe would come to follow Jesus. It became his life's work. Do what Jesus asks you to do. Don't start something else until He tells you to put the nets away. There is a catch for you or your successor that will only happen because you put the nets in, just one more time, **"for a catch."**

Saying "Yes" When Everything Within You Cries "No."

He took Peter and the two sons of Zebedee along with him, and he began to be sorrowful and troubled. Then he said to them, "My soul is overwhelmed with sorrow to the point of death. Stay here and keep watch with me."

Going a little farther, he fell with his face to the ground and prayed, "My Father, if it is possible, may this cup be taken from me. Yet not as I will, but as you will."

Then he returned to his disciples and found them sleeping. "Could you men not keep watch with me for one hour?" he asked Peter, "Watch and pray so that you will not fall into temptation. The spirit is willing, but the body is weak." Matthew 26:37-41

And being in anguish, he prayed more earnestly, and his sweat was like drops of blood falling to the ground. Luke 22:44

Jesus was headed for the cross. In less than twenty-four hours he would be dead. It would be a death at the hands of the masters of death. Professional soldiers who knew how to make a person suffer. The death would be a public spectacle so that it would be a lasting deterrent to anyone else who might consider breaking Roman law.

Jesus would know sin for the first time. It would not be His but the sin of everyone who had or would ever live. Their guilt, shame, and isolation from God would all be His. He knew all this as a human being. Just like you and me. He had to cope with it just like we would.

We will never face this specific decision. But ours will have some of the same characteristics. Dreams in our lives may have to die because they aren't God's will. Public humiliation may follow us as we hold to one of Christ's commands that isn't popular. We could get fired, undermined, demoted, or become the talk of the local rumor mill. As we accept responsibility for our own actions we could face criminal prosecution. At some point Christ's commands to us will not be what we want to put into practice.

At these points we will find ourselves where Christ was that night. In those times we need to do what Jesus did: pray. We need to hear the reassuring voice of God as He confirms His will for us. He will help us if we come to Him for help. **An angel from heaven appeared to him and strengthened him. Luke 22:43** Jesus got His help from an angel. You will get your help too.

Did that take the pain away from Jesus? No. He endured all that was thrown at Him, and it was all thrown at Him. Did it get any easier? No. But it became His decision; it became a part of HIS-story.

When everything within you is crying out "No" and you know that God is saying, "Yes," go with God's will and become a part of HIS-story.

Do Not Be Afraid

When evening came, the boat was in the middle of the lake, and he was alone on land. He saw the disciples straining at the oars, because the wind was against them. About the fourth watch of the night he went out to them, walking on the lake. He was about to pass by them, but when they saw him walking on the lake, they thought he was a ghost. They cried out, because they saw him and were terrified.

Immediately he spoke to them and said, "Take courage! It is I. Don't be afraid." Mark 6:47-50

Fear was an honest reaction from the disciples. It would be an honest reaction from any of us. In fact many of the spiritual encounters that can take place will have an initial reaction of fear. We are not used to this spiritual world that is out there. Sometimes following Jesus will put us right in the middle of it.

Why not fear? Fear is one step too close to panic. In situations where fear becomes the driving force, people can panic and do some very regrettable things. Once panic rules the situation anything can happen. People kill others, and themselves, they lie, cheat, steal, in short, they do things they would normally not even consider.

At that point we are not between the two white lines. We are on Satan's track between the two black lines of fear and hate. If you look at history you will see individuals and countries that walked between those lines. They ruled by fear and produced hate as a by-product.

So how do we avoid this detour? Jesus would have us replace the fear with peace. **On the evening of that first day of the week, when the disciples were together, with the doors locked for fear of the Jews, Jesus came and stood among them and said, "Peace be with you!" John 20:19** Jesus had been crucified and buried. Now He shows up out of nowhere, somehow getting past the locked doors. Fear would have been the honest reaction again. Instead, He gave us the antidote to fear: peace.

Peace will allow you to stay between the two white lines in all the actions and reactions to the circumstances of life. Peace becomes the standard that we need to maintain in our hearts. If we sense that fear is replacing peace, we need to spend some time with Jesus--right now. Whatever our circumstances are, we dare not react out of fear. **For God did not give us a spirit of timidity** [fear, in some versions], **but a spirit of power, of love and of self-discipline. 2 Timothy 1:7**

Fear can also lead to the most destructive behavior of all: avoiding God. If we are afraid of Him, we won't go to Him. If we don't go to Him, we end up off the road and then in our enemy's territory.

We can be afraid of Him because of our sin, failures, or what "we think" He is going to do. Instead of fear, Jesus has provided us with an open invitation to go into the throne room of God.

Therefore, since we have a great high priest who has gone through the heavens, Jesus the Son of God, let us hold firmly to the faith we profess. For we do not have a high priest who is unable to sympathize with our

weaknesses, but we have one who has been tempted in every way, just as we are--yet was without sin. Let us then approach the throne of grace with confidence, so that we may receive mercy and find grace to help us in our time of need. Hebrews 4:14-16

Fear paralyzes. Grace enables us to obey. Fear forces us to lose our focus. Mercy keeps us coming back to God. Fear is a warning sign to us that we need to draw near to the first white line. When fear is dealt with, we can do God's bidding. **Then Jesus said to Simon, "Don't be afraid; from now on you will catch men." Luke 5:10**

Lazarus, Come Out!

Gravity, the rising of the sun, weather, and death are all things that are a part of our lives. We may not like them, they may be inconvenient, but we have learned to accept them. They are so predictable that we can calculate the factors of gravity accurately enough to launch a rocket to Mars; and it gets there. A sunrise can be predicted to the minute. Weather is monitored and reported worldwide with any moment by moment changes. Death is inevitable.

When he had said this, Jesus called in a loud voice, "Lazarus, come out!" The dead man came out, his hands and feet wrapped with strips of linen, and a cloth around his face.

Jesus said to them, "Take off the grave clothes and let him go." John 11:43-44

Jesus has power over the forces of creation. He demonstrated it once again with Lazarus. He had already calmed a raging storm at sea with, **"Quiet! Be still!" (Mark 4:39)** Once He found a fruit tree without fruit and withered it with His words (Matthew 21:19) and for His first miracle He had changed water into wine. (John 2:1-11)

All of those predictable laws of nature seem to have exceptions. Jesus seems to have the power to rewrite the laws as needed. This makes sense when you realize that He was part of the creative team that birthed all of the forces and facets of nature and the universe that we know. **In the beginning God created the heavens and the earth. Genesis 1:1 For by him all things were created: things in heaven and on earth, visible and invisible, whether thrones or powers or rulers or authorities; all things were created by him and for him. He is before all things, and in him all things hold together. Colossians 1:16-17**

As His representatives and at His bidding, we can do what needs to be done despite the laws of nature that would govern us at any other time. **"I tell you the truth, if anyone says to this mountain, 'Go, throw yourself into the sea,' and does not doubt in his heart but believes that what he says will happen, it will be done for him." Mark 11:23** Obeying the voice of God in this area will have its own challenges. Peter began to walk on water (Matthew 14:28-31) in opposition to the laws of nature. He was successful as long as his faith was greater than his fear. When fear overcame the faith (Matthew 14:30) he was at the mercy of the creation.

How often, if ever, you will be called upon to action in this area is hard to say. Only God's specific plans for you will determine that. Rather than fear this area, know that if He speaks a word to your heart, you can speak the word to His creation. Don't go looking for the spectacular; let Him bring it to you.

You Deaf and Mute Spirit!

When Jesus saw that a crowd was running to the scene, he rebuked the evil spirit. "You deaf and mute spirit," he said, "I command you, come out of him and never enter him again."

The spirit shrieked, convulsed him violently and came out. The boy looked so much like a corpse that many said, "He's dead." But Jesus took him by the hand and lifted him to his feet, and he stood up. **Mark 9:25-27**

Demonic forces are a very real part of life. Biblically we are exposed to a number of behaviors and symptoms that are sometimes attributed to demons. As we look at them and how to minister to these people you will find that staying between the two white lines is the best preparation for this kind of ministry. It is a ministry that is dependent on your hearing God's voice and utilizing the guidelines that exist in scripture.

Let's start with a common problem, headaches, to illustrate our dependence on hearing God's voice and utilizing the guidelines of scripture. People can get headaches because they haven't had enough water in the day; that isn't demonic, just biological. It is God's built-in safeguard. We get a headache, slow down, drink some water, and we're O.K. You can pray for those people and it isn't a demonic issue. Don't neglect to tell them to drink some water after they are healed. God's mercy took the inconvenience away but He didn't change their built-in need for water.

Stress can also produce headaches. When we don't handle life's issues well we can see physical symptoms as a result. Again, this is not a demonic issue but a maturity issue. Prayer for the symptoms and advice for the lifestyle issues are appropriate here. They may need some on-going help to deal with the issues they are facing or they will face these kinds of headaches often.

Stress can also be the word that people use when they are really dealing with guilt. If God is convicting them of something and they are trying to ignore it, their symptoms will be very similar to stress that is not related to conviction. This conviction may be related to a sin they aren't dealing with or a decision they aren't making. So bringing them to a point of dealing with the issue is important before you see any kinds of results in this kind of setting.

Headaches can be caused by a new set of glasses that are too tight and restricting the blood flow to the brain. They can also be caused by a tumor that is doing the same thing. The tumor can have a number of origins; it could also be demonic.

You may have someone who is actively involved in the demonic world living in your home and that may be the cause of the headaches. I have seen every one of these examples and more. So how do you pray for a headache? You don't worry about the possibilities and your inability to properly diagnose the situation. You pray until you are in God's presence, ask enough questions until you can formulate a plan, and when you think you have a plan you ask God if that sounds right and then proceed if He doesn't give you a red light. We all know when God is saying no. We need to learn that He says yes too.

This example holds true for all of the physical symptoms that can be demonic as well as biological or related to personal neglect or immaturity. You will find in scripture that the same symptoms can have very different sources. So hear God's voice before you pull God's trigger.

If you are wrong you can leave the person you prayed for worse off than before you prayed. So take the time to pray until you have God's diagnosis for the issue before you issue the prescription.

When it is More than a Headache

When Jesus got out of the boat, a man with an evil spirit came from the tombs to meet him. This man lived in the tombs, and no one could bind him any more, not even with a chain. For he had often been chained hand and foot, but he tore the chains apart and broke the irons on his feet. No one was strong enough to subdue him. Night and day among the tombs and in the hills he would cry out and cut himself with stones. **Mark 5:2-5**

Demonic forces can be a part of this kind of behavior as well as seizures (Matthew 17:15-18), disease symptoms (Luke 13:10-13), suicidal actions (see above and John 10:10), lying (John 8:44), wrong ideas (Matthew 16:23) and a host of other destructive behaviors. Demons are contributing influences but they do not have the power to turn a person into something they don't choose to be. At this point you need to forget all the horror movies you have seen on this issue.

We do what we do based on the options we have (Romans 10:14-15). If I think revenge is an option, I may do something horrible. Newspapers are full of stories that illustrate this. So for the man from the tombs, the suicidal person, the liar, and those with wrong ideas (not just immaturity or mistakes) you will find people who had a thought and developed it into action. That thought wasn't from God and they didn't personally create it; it came from a demonic source. Demonic sources are very real and prevalent. If we look at our own thought life we will see that they offer suggestions on a regular basis.

But suggestions and action are two very different things. We are told to evaluate the thoughts we have (2 Corinthians 10:5) and only develop those from God (Galatians 5:23-26) into action.

Our physical health is impacted by the decisions we and others make. All of the physical symptoms that we have identified as being demonic can also be caused by the same factors that we discussed for a headache. So hearing God's voice before you pull God's trigger is still the proper advice. Physically, demonic forces can impact us when others or we give in to the suggestions and lifestyles they offer.

If your father became a satanic priest, you could be impacted physically. If you became bitter and envious because of the suggestions of demonic forces, you would eventually be physically impacted. Our prolonged exposure, agreement, and involvement with their suggestions is the starting point of this. It can be our choice or choices family members make before us.

So how do you deal with it? In every Biblical example the people who came to Jesus came under their own power. If they were brought to Jesus, it was by those who had rightful oversight for them. This is important because the power of Jesus is greater than the demonic forces, and through that power you can cast demons out of people.

You can also cast demons out of people who don't really want them to leave. For them your temporary show of power will ultimately leave them seven times worse than they were before.

"**When an evil spirit comes out of a man, it goes through arid places seeking rest and does not find it. Then it says, 'I will return to the house I left.' When it arrives, it finds the house unoccupied, swept clean and put in order. Then it goes and takes with it seven other spirits more wicked than itself, and they go in and live there. And the final condition of that man is worse than the first. That is how it will be with this wicked generation."** Matthew 12:43-45

Submit yourselves, then, to God. Resist the devil, and he will flee from you. Come near to God and he will come near to you. Wash your hands, you sinners, and purify your hearts, you double-minded. Grieve, mourn and wail. Change your laughter to mourning and your joy to gloom. Humble yourselves before the Lord, and he will lift you up. James 4:7-10

Those involved must want what God wants for them. That may mean a variety of actions on their part: repentance, confession, forgiveness, or more. If they submit to God by coming forward for prayer or by calling you, they are probably a candidate for a permanent deliverance. When you stumble on a situation or are brought in by well-meaning people you will have to evaluate the situation.

When it comes time to act, remember that you will only win this battle because of Jesus. You see Paul speaking these words, **"In the name of Jesus Christ I command you to come out of her!" At that moment the spirit left her.** Acts 16:18b This girl had followed Paul for days; now she could follow Jesus for a lifetime. Jesus sends you as His representative (Acts 19:13-16) to finish the work he made possible (1 John 3:8).

Realistically these kinds of things are best handled between people of the same gender and with more than one person present. Privacy is ideal and a Biblical explanation is always important for those involved. If problems develop or there is a resistance on the part of the demons (they can speak to you and say this), then you may have to go back to the submission issue with the people involved. Is this person ready to submit to God on this issue? If not, pray for them that they will come to that point and then leave them alone.

You can see that living between the two white lines is a prerequisite to effective ministry in this area. That is the only prerequisite. Knowing the scriptures is important and experience always helps, but your status on the road we are called to is more important that any title or position. When it is more than a headache remember whom you represent and what He did, and you can see the results He saw.

Healed

When he (Jesus) **came down from the mountainside, large crowds followed him. A man with leprosy came and knelt before him and said, "Lord, if you are willing, you can make me clean." Jesus reached out his hand and touched the man. "I am willing," he said, "Be clean!" Immediately he was cured of his leprosy. Matthew 8:1-3**

Sometimes He touched, other times He simply told them that they or the one they were concerned about was healed (Matthew 8:13). One blind man was told to go wash in a pool to receive his sight after Jesus had put mud on his eyes (John 9:6-7). Still another blind man received his sight after Jesus **"spit on the man's eyes and put his hands on him." Mark 8:23** That particular healing was accomplished in two phases. Jesus put His hands on the man twice before he saw clearly.

Dead people were raised to life by His command (John 11:43 and Luke 7:14). The crippled were healed when they responded to Christ's request (Mark 3:3). A lady who pushed through the crowd just to touch His garment was healed (Luke 8:43-48). People were healed from the worst diseases and the ultimate disease: death. It didn't take long to be healed and the Biblical accounts make it seem pretty easy and normal.

So where are the stories today? They still happen because Jesus is still the same (Hebrews 13:8). But because we are also still the same, we may go a long time before we see a verifiable healing.

"Lord, have mercy on my son," he said. "He has seizures and is suffering greatly. He often falls into the fire or into the water. I brought him to your disciples, but they could not heal him." Matthew 17:15-16 When the disciples came to Jesus in private and asked, "Why couldn't we drive it out? He replied, "Because you have so little faith." Matthew 17:19-20a Faith can be the issue for both the one praying and the one being prayed for. Is the faith born in their knowledge of God? Or are they only trying something? But faith is not the only issue that affects a ministry in healing.

Our personal preparation is often in shambles. We may not have spent any quality time with God for days, weeks, or months and we wonder why we don't have the right answers or see the healings. Without the open channels to God's heart and desire we won't know how to respond or act. Remember there are no formulas to memorize; Jesus did not leave us a pattern to follow. That puts us in complete reliance on God for the unique situation that every possible healing is.

When we looked at the demonic area of ministry, we had to look at stress, sin, personal neglect, immaturity, demonic influence and biological problems before we could take steps that will solve the problem, not just deal with the issue temporarily. It isn't any different for healings. Complex? So complex that you must rely on the relationship that Jesus made possible for you. If that is intact and functioning then it can seem as easy as it did in scripture. If not, then you will wonder as many do, "Why don't we see the healings?"

Home-Town Obstacles

As you can see, ministry has many exciting possibilities as well as some very practical obstacles. One that Jesus and you may face is the hometown obstacle. **Jesus said to them, "Surely you will quote this proverb to me: 'Physician, heal yourself! Do here in your hometown what we have heard that you did in Capernaum.'" "I tell you the truth," he continued, "no prophet is accepted in his hometown." Luke 4:23-24**

I have lived in the same town now for almost thirty years; it was over twenty years ago that I began to follow Jesus. Some remember me before I was a Christian and can't believe that I became one. Others remember me as a new Christian with lots of zeal and no maturity. Those that were around when I first began to minister tell great stories of my early attempts at preaching and life. All that is great history but unfortunately it also clouds the waters for ministry in my hometown. I am not Paul the apostle, but he faced the same trouble that Jesus did, I have, and you may. **When he came to Jerusalem, he tried to join the disciples, but they were all afraid of him, not believing that he really was a disciple. Acts 9:26**

Don't let this practical reality frustrate you or stop what God is doing in your life and the ministry that is developing as you live between the two white lines. God will provide opportunities for you as long as you can love the hometown that doesn't understand you. Pray that, in time, you will have the opportunities to minister where your heart has been raised.

Until that time comes, don't stop doing what you can wherever God leads you. That will prepare you for the time when you have some open doors of ministry at home.

Evangelism-Seekers

As Jesus started on his way, a man ran up to him and fell on his knees before him. "Good teacher," he asked, "what must I do to inherit eternal life?"

"Why do you call me good?" Jesus answered. "No one is good--except God alone. You know the commandments: Do not murder, do not commit adultery, do not steal, do not give false testimony, do not defraud, honor your father and mother."

"Teacher," he declared, "all these I have kept since I was a boy."

Jesus looked at him and loved him. "One thing you lack," he said. "Go, sell everything you have and give to the poor, and you will have treasure in heaven. Then come, follow me."

At this the man's face fell. He went away sad, because he had great wealth. Mark 10:17-22

People often came to Jesus with a form of this question: What do I do to be O.K. with God? They were seekers. Christ's love compelled Him to give the only true answer: Repent and obey me (see introduction). Unfortunately, many people have asked that same question and gotten a very different answer: Come as you are and add Jesus to your mess. Then when Jesus tries to change the mess, they struggle and finally walk away from Him because that wasn't in the original bargain.

People can't try Jesus. He isn't a sample at the bakery counter. They can dig into His teachings. They can consider His demands. They can ask questions. But if they are going to know Jesus and all He has for them, they must first repent, be forgiven, and then work with Him as they put His words into practice (Matthew 7:24-27).

We like to deal with people that are "seekers." Seekers come to us. We may be praying for them and may have planted some seed in their hearts but we want them to come to us. When that happens we assume that they are serious about Jesus. Too often we make the door to the Kingdom of God bigger than it really is and say come on in. That is generous but it is not love. That is easy but it isn't honest.

The doorway to the kingdom of God is one-man wide; Jesus made it for us with His life and death and resurrection. The only way you come into the Kingdom is through that door, that **"narrow gate" (Matthew 7:13-14)**; nothing else works.

You can't bring anything in with you. You can't sneak something in. Eventually you will have to deal with it. If you think you can sneak it in you have an unhealthy affection for something that will hurt you if you don't deal with it. For this man is was his wealth.

Jesus **"loved"** this man. We need to love all the seekers that come to our churches and to us. We need to love them enough to make possible all that God has for them. Tell them what Jesus told you: repent. Leave it all behind and let Jesus build the new you from the ground up. Spoken in love, that is love and that is honest.

Evangelism-Seek Them

After this, Jesus went out and saw a tax collector by the name of Levi sitting at his tax booth. "Follow me," Jesus said to him, and Levi got up, left everything and followed him. Luke 5:27-28 When Jesus reached the spot, he looked up and said to him, "Zacchaeus, come down immediately. I must stay at your house today." So he came down at once and welcomed him gladly.

All the people saw this and began to mutter, "He has gone to be the guest of a 'sinner.'"

But Zacchaeus stood up and said to the Lord, "Look, Lord!" Here and now I give half of my possessions to the poor, and if I have cheated anybody out of anything, I will pay back four times the amount."

Jesus said to him, "Today salvation has come to this house, because this man, too, is a son of Abraham. For the Son of Man came to seek and to save what was lost. Luke 19:5-10

Tax collectors were some of the most despised people in Israel. Dishonest and disloyal to the Jewish race, they made their living exploiting everyone through a crooked taxing system. Jesus went out of his way to offer the new life to these and many other despised people. People who would never be welcomed as "seekers".

Our evangelistic efforts need to include ways to reach the despised people in our cultures. Despised people don't become a "seeker". They know they are despised. If we don't, large groups of people will never seek us. Whole countries will never seek us. That is why we **"love our enemies,"** so that in time we will have the opportunity to seek them.

Seeking out the despised and ignored is a growing task here in America. For decades we have assumed that everyone at least knew about the Gospel but some had chosen to ignore it. We were wrong. Now we are facing a generation that has very little accurate information about Jesus and His people.

As you live your life learn to seek the despised, the ignored, the Gospel "challenged" people that are all around you. When you do, you will begin to understand a part of Jesus' heart that so few do. Why did the **"Son of Man"** come? **"To seek and to save what was lost."** You will never have that heart for yourself until you go and do what He did for them.

Mercy Ministry

During those days another large crowd gathered. Since they had nothing to eat, Jesus called his disciples to him and said, "I have compassion for these people; they have already been with me three days and have nothing to eat. If I send them home hungry, they will collapse on the way, because some of them have come a long distance."

His disciples answered, "But where in this remote place can anyone get enough bread to feed them?"

"How many loaves do you have?" Jesus asked.

"Seven," they replied.

He told the crowd to sit down on the ground. When he had taken the seven loaves and given thanks, he broke them and gave them to his disciples to set before the people, and they did so. They had a few small fish as well; he gave thanks for them also and told the disciples to distribute them. The people ate and were satisfied. Mark 8:1-8a

In Joppa there was a disciple named Tabitha (which, when translated, is Dorcas), who was always doing good and helping the poor. About that time she became sick and died, and her body was washed and placed in an upstairs room. Lydda was near Joppa; so when the disciples heard that Peter was in Lydda, they sent two men to him and urged him, "Please come at once!"

Peter went with them, and when he arrived he was taken upstairs to the room. All the widows stood around him, crying and showing him the robes and other clothing that Dorcas had made while she was still with them. Acts 9:36-39

Feeding the hungry and clothing those without has been a part of ministry since the very beginning of the church. It comes from the compassion that Christ has for people. Today we call these types of ministries, mercy ministries. Ministering to people who can't, haven't, or won't take care of themselves is compassion and pre-evangelism as well.

It can take many forms. Building homes, administering medical work, digging wells and latrines, training people for jobs, running feeding programs and clothing banks, teaching child-raising classes and language courses and caring for the elderly are just a few of the many ways the mercy of God can be extended by His people.

Mercy ministries can be extended to people in your hometown, victims of natural disasters, and refugees from wars that rage worldwide. The opportunity for mercy ministries is endless. You can give to or work for an organization. You can pray for their work, coordinate evangelistic efforts, or start something where there is a need.

Mercy flows from God through His people. Remember His mercy will always include the opportunity to hear the Gospel. Feeding war-torn refugees is great. Telling them about Jesus so they don't hate their oppressors and seek a revenge war makes the mercy complete.   Clothing street people is great but stopping there only means you have warm street people.   Their hearts will be just as cold as they were before you gave them a coat.

It has been said that you can feed a man a fish and take away his hunger for a day or you can take a day to teach a man to fish and he will be well fed for the rest of his life.   Our mercy needs to take the second line of action whenever possible: Introduce the Gospel.

Others-Unity

"Master," said John, "we saw a man driving out demons in your name and we tried to stop him, because he is not one of us."

"Do not stop him," Jesus said, "for whoever is not against you is for you." Luke 9:49-50

It is even a bigger question today than it was for John. Our phone books are full of organizations that are listed as churches. How many of them would Jesus give His stamp of approval to? Within Jesus' answer to John we find our answer for today, too.

What this **"man"** was doing is the key then and is still the key today. This **"man"** was fulfilling one of the ministries that Jesus has made possible for us. Jesus gives His power to those who are His to accomplish His work. Just using the name of Jesus like a stolen credit card won't get the work done.

Some Jews who went around driving out evil spirits tried to invoke the name of the Lord Jesus over those who were demon-possessed. They would say, "In the name of Jesus, whom Paul preaches, I command you to come out." Seven sons of Sceva, a Jewish chief priest, were doing this. [One day] the evil spirit

answered them, "Jesus I know, and I know about Paul, but who are you?" Then the man who had the evil spirit jumped on them and overpowered them all. He gave them such a beating that they ran out of the house naked and bleeding. **Acts 19:13-16**

Churches can have many different names. If they are doing what Jesus commanded them to do the way He commanded them to do it then, **"Do not stop"** them. In fact it would be good to get to know them so you can work together. Working together, you can always accomplish more than you can by yourself.

You will always have differences. Cultures, backgrounds, gifting, and opinions can make us seem very different. However, if we are both working on Christ's commands, we are driving down the same highway and will end up in the same place. I can be a Godly Christian man and wear a skirt in some countries and slacks somewhere else. I can worship with every instrument invented in one building and use only voices in another and still worship in spirit and in truth.

If, however, I delete Christ's commands from my lifestyle and invent another way other than Jesus' way to be acceptable to God then I am not a fellow worker. I need to hear the Gospel as much as any lost tribe in the jungle, even if the name of my church sounds like yours.

Confusing? It can be. Many countries invent new religions on a daily basis, attempting to fill the void that only Christ can eliminate. Some of these are the result of ignorance; they haven't heard the truth and are doing the best they can with what they have. Others are acting in rebellion; they don't like what Jesus said so they are writing their own books and life script.

Looking at people with these questions in mind will help you to understand if they are for or against Jesus. First, have they substituted something or someone else for

Jesus (John 14:6)? If Jesus alone isn't Savior and Lord, you need to question their intentions. Secondly, if they aren't honest about sin (Romans 3:23 & 6:23) and what sin is (Bible lists) then you need to watch out. Third, if they have other books that are more important than the Bible then they hold the potential to be against you. Fourth, do they rely on and look for the power that God offers to live their lives (Acts 1:8) or do they do it in their own strength? These are four questions that will allow you to know if you should consider them as co-workers.

Time will also tell you a lot about an organization. What kind of people come from that organization? What is the reputation in the community? These are all things to consider. Unfortunately, you will also see real churches that are struggling because of immaturity and division in the organization. They aren't disqualified from Christ's kingdom but they aren't helping to build it, either.

Start with the samples from scripture and ask the four questions. From that point you can begin to know who your partners are and who still needs to hear the Gospel. **"My prayer is not for them alone. I pray also for those who will believe in me through their message, that all of them may be one, Father, just as you are in me and I am in you. May they also be in us so that the world may believe that you have sent me." John 17:20-21**

Woe to Religion

"Woe to you Pharisees, because you give God a tenth of your mint, rue and all other kinds of garden herbs, but you neglect justice and the love of God. You should have practiced the latter without leaving the former undone." Luke 11:42

Jesus was warning people who had chosen to follow some of God's commands but not all of them. They were "religious." By definition, "religion" is a system of thought, feeling, and action shared by a group. When this system includes only a partial list of God's commands, watch out. People who practice this religion can make a good first impression but aren't living between the two white lines.

Watch out for these people. They aren't ready to become your co-workers yet. Watch for this in yourself, too. Some of Christ's commands will be easier for you to obey than others. That doesn't mean they aren't for you to obey. It only means you will have to draw nearer to Jesus to get those tough ones accomplished.

"Woe to you Pharisees, because you love the most important seats in the synagogues and greetings in the marketplaces." Luke 11:43 Impressing others can give you some special attention. It happens in the sport and entertainment world and it can happen in the Church world too. When this special attention becomes a goal in the Church world then we have lost sight of one of Christ's commands; **Sitting down, Jesus called the Twelve and said, "If anyone wants to be first, he must be the very last, and the servant of all." Mark 9:35**

Receiving special attention is a blessing. Seeking special attention is a sign of immaturity. Religious groups tend to have a system that you become a part of and receive special attention and titles. Jesus avoided all of that as He ate what everyone else ate and stayed where everyone else stayed and did what He asked everyone else to do. **Jesus replied, "And you experts in the law, woe to you, because you load people down with burdens they can hardly carry, and you yourselves will not lift one finger to help them." Luke 11:46**

You will find religions and religious people all over the world. They may be very devoted and do admirable things. Devotion and admirable works are all good things. But if they are not God's things then Jesus would not praise them and neither can we. **"Woe to you experts in the law, because you have taken away the key to knowledge. You yourselves have not entered, and you have hindered those who were entering." Luke 11:52**

Jesus knew that people needed the guidelines that He gave in His commands to live life the way it was intended to be lived. Life between the two white lines gives us our relationship with God and the tools for a relationship with people. Religions don't; they can't do that. They become places where the **"key to knowledge"** is lost among the rules and rituals of the organization. So watch out for rules and any religious behavior that might be developed to cover over or avoid any of the commands Christ has left us to obey.

The Sabbath

Another time he went into the synagogue, and a man with a shriveled hand was there. Some of them were looking for a reason to accuse Jesus, so they watched him closely to see if he would heal him on the Sabbath. Jesus said to the man with the shriveled hand, "Stand up in front of everyone."

Then Jesus asked them, "Which is lawful on the Sabbath: to do good or to do evil, to save life or to kill?" But they remained silent

He looked around at them in anger and, deeply distressed at their stubborn hearts, said to the man, "Stretch out your hand." He stretched it out, and his hand was completely restored. Then the Pharisees went out and began to plot with the Herodians how they might kill Jesus. Mark 3:1-6

God used the seventh day (Genesis 2:2-3) to rest; He set that day aside for us as well and it is called the Sabbath. Unfortunately, this day of rest had become so religious by the time Jesus came that there was more tension about the day than there was rest. People had created hundreds of religious rules that were supposed to be obeyed in order to have a Godly Sabbath. There were so many rules that it became a sin to **"do good;"** to heal on the Sabbath.

In many of the churches that I am in (as an evangelist I visit about sixty different churches a year and several different countries) they have added rules to their code of conduct that are there to prevent a problem from repeating itself. Sometimes these rules prevent one problem but create another. Other times these rules are reactions to issues that don't apply anymore but are still enforced.

In one of those countries I ministered in people are met with a list of what they can wear, where they can go, and what they can and can't do as soon as they come to church. The list was created decades ago. It should have been destroyed decades ago. The list doesn't help you to stay between the two white lines; it only makes you look like a clone of the group. You don't please God anymore if you keep the list you only make the group feel good about themselves. The rules aren't found in scripture; instead they were written by people who apparently didn't know the scriptures very well. It puts an unnecessary strain on people, like the Sabbath laws that Jesus faced.

When you are tempted to make rules about Christian living that aren't found in scripture, beware of this trap. We are faced with hundreds of decisions every day. Making rules to avoid these decisions can seem like a short cut but it really cuts your throat in the long run. Jesus gave us all the rules we need. Use them to make your decisions and you will produce the right outcome. Each situation is so complex and different that it becomes very hard to achieve justice and mercy with our rules and regulations. Only Jesus had the heart and wisdom to make that possible for us in the commands He left behind.

If we insist on adding our ink to the TWO WHITE LINES we will find ourselves narrowing the lane, sometimes to the point that it becomes a tight wire that none can walk.

We are commanded to rest from our work on the Sabbath. We need rest. We need the time to refocus on Christ and His commands. We need the seventh day of the week to get ready for the first day of the next week. We need it whether we think so or not. Like any command, our obedience at this point will make our obedience later that much easier. Rested people respond better to the strain of life than those who have never taken the time to observe the Sabbath.

Forgiveness From God

Justice and forgiveness always seem to compete for the same space. Every courtroom knows the tension of the prosecution who pushes for the maximum sentence and the defense that pleads for the mercy of the court. It is a drama that is played out daily in our legal system and everyday life. What punishment should be paid by those who do wrong? It was one of the key struggle points for the religious people of Jesus' time. It is still one of the areas where religious people struggle today.

One day as he was teaching, Pharisees and teachers of the law, who had come from every village of Galilee and from Judea and Jerusalem, were sitting there. And the power of the Lord was present for him to heal the sick. Some men came carrying a paralytic on a mat and tried to take him into the house to lay him before Jesus. When they could not find a way to do this because of the crowd, they went up on the roof and lowered him on his mat through the tiles into the middle of the crowd, right in front of Jesus.

When Jesus saw their faith, he said, "Friend, your sins are forgiven."

The Pharisees and the teachers of the law began thinking to themselves, "Who is this fellow who speaks blasphemy? Who can forgive sins but God alone?"

Jesus knew what they were thinking and asked, "Why are you thinking these things in your hearts? Which is easier: to say, 'Your sins are forgiven,' or to say, 'Get up and walk?' But that you may know that the Son of Man has authority on earth to forgive sins...." He said to the paralyzed man, "I tell you, get up, take your mat and go home." Immediately he stood up in front of them, took what he had been lying on and went home praising God. Luke 5:17-24

No longer a paralytic; no longer a sinner. What a day for that man and what a struggle for the religious. Jesus forgave just as He forgives today. His work on the cross was the ultimate tension point in history. Justice and forgiveness occupied the same space. From that date forward, our repentance will clear the way for Christ's forgiveness. We need to help the religious find that forgiveness.

Today that can seem too easy, even unfair. What about murders and rapists? What Jesus did was so long ago now. The religious can struggle. If you find yourself struggling to forgive others or yourself, you have forgotten what Jesus did for the world that Father God loves. You have forgotten the gruesome punishment that Jesus experienced at the hands of His captors, before and during the cross. You have forgotten the emotional weight of the world's sin, as Jesus was pronounced guilty for all of it. Most likely you have forgotten the freedom that forgiveness brings.

Ministering to those caught in the religious trap of un-forgiveness requires that you have had recent experience in forgiveness. Your heart needs to have won the battle of justice and forgiveness. Then you will have what it takes to rescue the religious.

Brothers, if someone is caught in a sin, you who are spiritual should restore him gently. But watch yourself, or you also may be tempted. Galatians 6:1 If we confess our sins, he is faithful and just and will forgive us our sins and purify us from all unrighteousness. 1 John 1:9

Doubting, Again

Now Thomas (called Didymus), one of the Twelve, was not with the disciples when Jesus came. When the other disciples told him that they had seen the Lord, he declared, "Unless I see the nail marks in his hands and put my finger where the nails were, and put my hand into his side, I will not believe it."

A week later his disciples were in the house again, and Thomas was with them. Though the doors were locked, Jesus came and stood among them and said, "Peace be with you!" Then he said to Thomas, "Put your finger here; see my hands. Reach out your hand and put it into my side. Stop doubting and believe." **John 20:24-27**

Then the eleven disciples went to Galilee, to the mountain where Jesus had told them to go. When they saw him, they worshipped him; but some doubted. **Matthew 28:16-17**

Doubt, that wavering emotion that causes you to throw out everything you know and have experienced for something else. Thomas had seen all the miracles, performed them himself (Luke 9:1-6), and still we find him doubting. We find ourselves doubting, too. We will find others doubting as well.

Jesus dealt with doubt; He didn't ignore it. These guidelines will help us as we deal with it and as we minister to those caught in it. Thomas doubted; thus the phrase, "Doubting Thomas." Jesus confronted that doubt by meeting the request with a specific reply. The fact that Thomas opened up and spoke about the area of doubt is the first key. We have to be honest before God, even if it means we doubt. He can handle that.

Next, we need to give God an opportunity to reply. Thomas stayed in the fellowship of the disciples for a week even though they had seen Jesus and he hadn't. If doubt were just an excuse for another issue then he would have left. Instead, doubt was an honest emotion as he was trying to deal with all the changes that Christ's death and resurrection brought.

Doubt also dissolves when you can do something about the focus of your emotion. In Matthew 28:18-20 Jesus gave the doubters something to do: **"Go!"** That would erase the foundation that doubt was standing on. It is still true for us today. Doubt loses out when we get a chance to see a fresh exhibit of God's love, power, and purposes in our lives. Making a phone call, praying, asking for help, spending some time working on a project, can shake you loose from the doubt that can paralyze progress in your life.

When you are ministering to those in doubt, remember these principles. It can be as easy as praying together. It may take some time and involvement. But whatever it takes, we are in good company with Jesus when we minister to those who become paralyzed by doubt.

If They Hate You

"If the world hates you, keep in mind that it hated me first. If you belonged to the world, it would love you as its own. As it is, you do not belong to the world, but I have chosen you out of the world. That is why the world hates you." John 15:18-19

"All this I have told you so that you will not go astray. They will put you out of the synagogue; in fact, a time is coming when anyone who kills you will think he is offering a service to God. They will do such things because they have not known the Father or me. I told you this, so that when the time comes you will remember that I warned you first because I was with you." John 16:1-4

Hate is a strong word. No one wants to be hated. Yet, it will happen. It can occur at work when you won't lie. If someone asks you to cheat for them at school and you say "no" you may be hated. Your testimony at a trial may send someone to jail; you could be hated. All these are possible.

Your opportunities to be hated increase, as you are involved in ministry that includes sharing the Gospel. Only then have I had rocks, curses, and a knife hurled my way. Only then has my life been threatened.

Don't be surprised. Jesus gave us this set of commands to remind us that we can be doing everything correctly and still face all kinds of opposition, even hatred. He did. How you handle hatred will depend on how comfortable you are with it. Being warned helps. It also helps us to know that even in the worst of it He has made a way for us to deal with it.

"Whenever you are arrested and brought to trial, do not worry beforehand about what to say. Just say whatever is given you at the time, for it is not you speaking, but the Holy Spirit." Mark 13:11 Hatred happens. Sometimes the Gospel will initiate hatred. Ultimately only the Gospel can eliminate it. When it happens know that you are loved so much by God that He sent His Son to be hated so you could be loved forever.

Tough Times Ahead

Jesus left the temple and was walking away when his disciples came up to him to call his attention to its buildings. "Do you see all these things?" he asked. "I tell you the truth, not one stone here will be left on another; every one will be thrown down." Matthew 24:1-2

We long for stability and peace. It affords us the opportunity to pursue our dreams and satisfy our desires without the threats of change. Jesus said it to His disciples then and would say to us now, tough times are ahead. Change is inevitable and it will be through some of the most violent ways imaginable.

"You will hear of wars and rumors of wars, but see to it that you are not alarmed. Such things must happen, but the end is still to come. Nations will rise against nation, and kingdom against kingdom. There will be famines and earthquakes in various places. All these are the beginning of birth pains." Matthew 24:6-8

Fortunately for us we can be "fishers of men" in any political, economic, or military climate. Yes, it will change our strategies, the tools we have to use, and some of the attitudes of people. But we have job security no matter what. Until the job is done we need to continue in the ministry we are called to.

"Then you will be handed over to be persecuted and put to death, and you will be hated by all nations because of me. At that time many will turn away from the faith and will betray and hate each other, and many false prophets will appear and deceive many people. Because of the increase in wickedness, the love of most will grow cold, but he who stands firm to the end will be saved. And this gospel of the kingdom will be preached in the whole world as a testimony to all nations, and then the end will come." Matthew 24:9-14

If we have a more favorable climate then we should be able to get more done and have more resources available to accomplish it. In a prison cell we will find our ministry is focused on guards and prayer and fasting. Each extreme has its own obstacles and unique opportunities. **"Stand firm."** Jesus commands us to do that no matter how tough our times are. He understands our situation more than we remember.

Consider him who endured such opposition from sinful men, so that you will not grow weary and lose heart. In your struggle against sin, you have not yet resisted to the point of shedding your blood. Hebrews 12:3-4

Quitting Time

After he said this, he was taken up before their eyes, and a cloud hid him from their sight. They were looking intently up into the sky as he was going, when suddenly two men dressed in white stood beside them. "Men of Galilee," they said "why do you stand here looking into the sky? This same Jesus, who has been taken from you into heaven, will come back in the same way you have seen him go into heaven." Acts 1:9-11

Border towns between the United States and Mexico can be fairly rough and ragged. This one was no exception and we were ministering in the part of town where all the bars and prostitution were. It was a Friday night. Very loud music attacked our ears, bathroom smells were everywhere, and our reception for sharing the Gospel was less than friendly. So it was easy to understand why the teams usually wanted to quit and go home before the appointed time.

Team members would begin to come to me and ask what time it was. Next, their trips out ministering would be of shorter duration. Finally, they would ask if they could go to the vans early. My response was usually, "No." Until we had reached the appointed time we weren't done. Once we reached it we were free to go and to celebrate what had been accomplished.

If I could keep a team motivated it was almost certain that someone who had come to the street scene to sin would accept Christ instead. But it always happened in the last fifteen minutes. Experience had shown us that working till the appointed time brought the results we had prayed for.

"No one knows about that day or hour, not even the angels in heaven, nor the Son, but only the Father. As it was in the days of Noah, so it will be at the coming of the Son of Man. For in the days before the flood, people were eating and drinking, marrying and giving in marriage, up to the day Noah entered the ark; and they knew nothing about what would happen until the flood came and took them all away. That is how it will be at the coming of the Son of Man." Matthew 24:36-39

We don't know when Jesus is coming back. It could happen before I finish ....this sentence. It could also be another decade or century. So how do we minister knowing that at some point it all stops? **"Who then is the faithful and wise servant, whom the master has put in charge of the servants in his household to give them their food at the proper time? It will be good for that servant whose master finds him doing so when he returns. I tell you the truth, he will put him in charge of all his possessions." Matthew 24:45-46**

Stopping before the appointed time would mean wasted time and ministry that never took place; people that won't hear. We don't stop until Jesus gives us the signal. He will. For each of us He will establish times of rest (Mark 6:31) and He has given us the Sabbath for rest. Ministry and life is not a frantic high speed flailing, it is at His command and lived at His pace (Galatians 5:25). But it is lived out until we die. We may minister in a variety of ways but we will minister until quitting time--if we are listening to the boss.

"But suppose that servant is wicked and says to himself, 'My master is staying away a long time,' and he then begins to beat his fellow servants and to eat and drink with drunkards. The master of that servant will come on a day when he does not expect him and at an hour he is not aware of. He will cut him to pieces and assign him a place with the hypocrites, where there will be weeping and gnashing of teeth." Matthew 24:48-51

In the midst of talking about His return Jesus gave the ultimate warning to His people. This warning will help us in all areas of ministry and life. **"Remember Lot's wife." Luke 17:32**

Genesis chapter 19 records the story of Lot and his family. God had blessed them in many ways. Lot had traveled with Abraham and their flocks became so large there wasn't enough food for them so Lot stayed behind near the city of Sodom. It was a fruitful lush valley. Sodom was the city closest to Lot. In time Lot and his family moved into Sodom and began to adopt its ways.

Sodom was not a good town to learn from. We get our word sodomy from this town. **Now the men of Sodom were wicked and were sinning greatly against the Lord. Genesis 13:13 Before they had gone to bed, all the men from every part of the city of Sodom--both young and old--surrounded the house. They called to Lot, "Where are the men who came to you tonight? Bring them out to us so we can have sex with them." Genesis 19:4-5**

God's mercy finally ran out on this area and He sent some angels to Lot to warn him that He was going to destroy this town and Gomorrah as well. These angels had to drag Lot and his family out of the city and gave stern warnings to them as they left; "Don't look back!" **But**

Lot's wife looked back, and she became a pillar of salt. Genesis 19:26

Lot's wife became a warning from that point on. Don't look back at the old life and ways when God has given you a chance for a new life. Going forward with God can mean leaving a comfortable situation behind. It will always mean change. The longer you live your life between the two white lines the more you will have to pass on. Your responsibility levels in the Kingdom of God may increase and that may mean change.

"Remember Lot's wife." Her comfort and the things she had grown accustomed to meant more to her than obedience to God. Finish your race well. Complete what God has set out for you. Don't let the blessings of God keep you from His promises.

As you learn the commandments that Christ left for us you will minister in a powerful way to those you meet. You may never leave your hometown or you may be sent around the world. Your location isn't important; your obedience is. You will also find that you end up accomplishing something with your lifetime that Jesus predicted for you. **"I tell you the truth, anyone who has faith in me will do what I have been doing. He will do even greater things than these, because I am going to the Father."** John 14:12

Christ's ministry ended when He was in His early thirties. You may live much longer than that. Christ never left His local area; the world is available to you. Jesus had to be wherever He was to minister. You can write books, record radio and TV messages, and send E-mail around the world. With a phone call you can change a life. Don't look back, give up, or slow down until the Boss calls it quits.

Baptize and Teach

"Therefore go and make disciples of all nations, baptizing them in the name of the Father and of the Son and of the Holy Spirit, and teaching them to obey everything I have commanded you." Matthew 28:19-20a

Baptism is a declaration to the world that someone has repented and is going to build the rest of their lives around all that the Father, Son, and Holy Spirit have for them. It is also just the starting place. Next we need to teach them everything that Christ has commanded them. Celebrate the baptism but then role up your sleeves and get ready for the work that is ahead.

Traveling as an evangelist I encounter situations where I get asked to preach on very short notice. When I only have minutes to prepare, certain themes and topics always come out. They are the things that are most important to me; the things I understand best. It is also very easy to only teach what you know best. We need to make sure we develop ways of teaching all of Christ's commands and putting them into practice.

New disciples need to be exposed to everything that Jesus has commanded us to teach. We need to be exposed to everything that Jesus has commanded us to teach. If we aren't exposed to His teachings we will have huge stretches of unpaved highway. If we don't review all of His commandments on a regular basis then parts of our highway will fall into disrepair.

The word disciple means that discipline will be involved. We need that discipline so we don't miss all that God has for each one of us with His commandments.

This book is written to help anyone who is trying to live and teach Christ's commands. As we apply His commands to our lives we will be able to teach others to do the same; **"teaching them to obey everything I have commanded you."**

Last Thoughts

Jesus left us with the words of life. Compiling them was a fresh way for me to deal with these commands in my own life. If you take the time you will find they will revitalize life. Don't become discouraged by your progress; just don't stop. Let others help you. Get into or stay in a good Bible based church. Don't try to be a Lone Ranger. You will have unique gifts and talents and experiences that are intended to benefit others. They will also help cover your weaknesses with their gifts and talents and unique experiences.

Jesus really did come to offer us life; **"I have come that they may have life, and have it to the full." John 10:10b** Build the highway on the cleared land that repentance brings. Live your life between the two white lines and it will challenge you and satisfy you like nothing else can. Thank you Jesus!

Scripture Reference Section

OLD TESTAMENT

Genesis
13:13 (239)
19:4-5 (239)
19:26 (240)

Exodus
34:29 (101)

Numbers
18:21 (78)
18:23-24 (78)
18:25-28 (78)
18:28 (78)

Dueteronomy
33:12 (181)

2 Samuel
11:1 (95)
12:11-12 (113)

1 Kings
21:4 (128)
21:27-29 (66)

2 Kings
6:23 (105)

Nehemiah
1:4 (66)

2:4-6 (66)

Psalms
51:16-17 (65)
66:3 (88)
102:4 (58)

Proverbs
19:11 (127)
28:19 (38)

Isaiah
40:30-31 (65,171)
58:6-7 (62)

Jeremiah
19:5-6 (174)

Daniel
10:3 (61)

Joel
2:12-13 (58)

Zechariah
7:2-5 (59)

NEW TESTAMENT

Matthew
4:10 (82)

Matthew

4:17 (165)
5:9 (133)
5:11-12 (152)
5:14 (97)
5:16 (101)
5:21-23 (126)
5:23-26 (149)
5:28 (95, 112)
5:33-37 (155)
5:38-42 (73)
5:42 (144)
5:47 (134)
5:48 (104)
6:2 (69)
6:2-4 (75,145)
6:5 (45)
6:6 (46)
6:7-8 (47)
6:9-13 (49)
6:14-15 (51)
6:16 (56)
6:16-18 (60)
6:18 (64)
6:19-21 (145)
6:24 (68)
6:33(95)
7:12 (117)
7:24-25 (11,14)
8:1-3 (206)
9:16-17 (56)
10:7-8 (175)
10:8 (179)
10:14 (153)
11:28-30 (37)

Matthew

12:33-37 (156)
12:43-45 (204)
12:50 (43)
13:22 (146)
13:43 (100)
13:57-58 (54)
14:15-21 (182)
14:29-31 (14)
16:16-17 (15)
16:22-23 (15)
16:23 (187)
17:1-2 (100)
17:15-16 (207)
17:19-20 (207)
18:5-6 (168)
18:10 (169)
18:15-17 (150)
18:21-22 (141)
18:23-35 (142)
19:3-9 (120)
22:14 (172)
22:36-40 (26)
22:37 (29)
22:39 (107)
24:1-2 (235)
24:6-8 (235)
24:9-14 (98,236)
24:14 (99)
24:36-39 (238)
24:45-46 (238)
24:48-51 (239)
24:45-51 (43)
26:37-41 (192)
26:39-41 (90)

Matthew

    28:16-17 (231)
    28:16-20 (176)
    28:19-20
    (5,232,241)

Mark

    1:17 (40)
    3:1-6 (225)
    3:3-6 (132)
    4:39 (197)
    5:2-5 (202)
    6:4-6 (183)
    6:31 (185)
    6:47-50 (194)
    8:1-8 (216)
    8:23 (206)
    8:36 (111)
    8:38 (17)
    9:23-24 (102)
    9:25-27 (199)
    9:25-29 (67)
    9:35 (223)
    10:13-14 (167)
    10:17-22 (211)
    10:25 (111)
    10:35 (147)
    10:37 (147)
    10:41-45 (147)
    11:23 (198)
    11:22-24 (53)
    12:30 (109)
    12:31 (115)
    13:11 (234)
    14:26 (82)

Mark

    14:66-72 (16)

Luke

    3:3-6 (10)
    3:11 (69)
    4:8 (87)
    4:23-24 (209)
    5:1-8 (190)
    5:10 (196)
    5:17-24 (229)
    5:27-28 (214)
    6:20-23 (160)
    6:24-26 (158)
    6:27-36 (124)
    6:37-38 (136)
    6:42 (139)
    7:47 (143)
    8:8 (30)
    8:13-14 (35)
    8:18 (31)
    9:23 (44)
    9:49-50 (219)
    9:54-56 (177)
    10:17-20 (178)
    10:41-42 (44)
    11:42 (222)
    11:43 (223)
    11:46 (223)
    11:52 (223)
    12:47 (172)
    13:22-24 (97)
    14:8-11 (148)
    14:12-14 (180)
    16:22-26 (183)

Luke

17:32 (239)
19:5-10 (214)
19:9-10 (39)
19:10 (134,180)
21:28 (101)
22:39-44 (34)
22:43 (193)
22:44 (192)
23:34 (105,125)
23:47 (125)
24:34 (17)
24:49 (170)

John

4:21-24 (84)
5:19 (179)
6:60 (31)
6:66 (31)
6:67-69 (31)
7:24 (137)
8:7 (138)
10:10 (243)
11:43-44 (197)
12:49 (135)
13:29 (69)
13:34 (118)
14:6 (40,97)
14:11-12 (184)
14:12 (103,240)
14:12-14 (102)
14:26 (5)
14:27 (33)
14:31 (32,164)
15:5 (173)

John

15:14-15 (43)
15:18-19 (233)
16:1-3 (154)
16:1-4 (233)
16:33 (125)
17:18 (41)
17:20-21 (221)
20:19 (195)
20:24-27 (231)
21:22 (163)

Acts

1:9-11 (237)
2:11 (17)
2:38 (166)
2:38-41 (17)
2:44-45 (69)
4:12 (39)
9:26 (209)
9:36-39 (217)
13:2 (64)
16:18 (204)
17:30 (166)
19:13-16
(178,220)
27:25 (24)

Romans

3:23 (137)
5:3-5 (77)
6:23 (12,13,173)
8:5 (57)
8:15-16 (46)
10:14 (41)

Romans
    10:14-15 (80)
    10:17 (23)
    12:2 (99)

1 Corinthians
    10:12-13 (94)
    15:9-10 (19,21)

2 Corinthians
    1:3-4 (156)
    1:8-11 (109)
    5:7 (24)
    5:17-20 (134)

2 Corinthians
    5:20 (177)
    6:16 (83)
    8:1-4 (76)
    8:13-15 (71)
    9:6 (80)
    9:7 (76)
    12:7-10 (19)

Galatians
    5:7 (26)
    5:16-18 (90)
    5:25 (57,62)
    6:1 (230)
    6:1-2 (151)
    6:9 (38)

Ephesians
    2:10 (11)
    2:20-22 (83)
    4:15 (131,137)

Ephesians
    4:26-27 (127)

Philippians
    1:4-6 (157)
    1:6 (146)
    2:29-30 (79)

Colossians
    1:16-17 (198)

1 Thessalonians
    4:3-7 (113)
    5:16-18 (52,88)

1 Timothy
    6:10 (110)

2 Timothy
    1:7 (195)

Titus
    1:16 (152)

Hebrews
    2:17-18 (94)
    4:14-16(34,196)
    4:16 (20,46)
    11:1 (64)
    11:1-2 (22)
    12:1-3 (28)
    12:3-4 (236)
    12:10-11 (15)
    12:11 (156)
    12:14 (149)

Hebrews
>   12:15 (150)
>   13:5 (72)
>   13:8 (103)

James
>   1:5 (130,150)
>   1:13-15 (89)
>   3:1 (187)
>   4:7-10 (96,204)

1 Peter
>   2:11 (57)
>   2:15 (79)

2 Peter
>   3:9 (40)

1 John
>   1:9 (95,230)
>   2:15-16 (92)
>   3:17 (69)
>   4:16 (108)
>   4:18 (156)
>   4:19 (108)
>   4:20-21 (105)

Revelation
>   3:19-22 (188)
>   4:10-11 (88)